Puppy Training for a Good Dog

A Guide to Raising a Good Dog and Caring for Your Furry Friend

Kevin Jobson

contained within this document, including, but not limited to, errors, omissions, or inaccuracies.

Table of Contents

INTRODUCTION 1

CHAPTER 1: WHEN IT ALL BEGAN 5

    THE EVOLUTION OF THE CANINE SPECIES 6
    THE HISTORICAL IMPACT OF THE CANINE SPECIES 9
    HOW THIS HAS AFFECTED DOG TRAINING 12

CHAPTER 2: BEFORE GETTING A DOG 15

    WHAT IS NEEDED 16
    SPEAK WITH YOUR FAMILY FIRST 18
    PREPARING YOUR HOME 19
    WHAT TRAINING DO YOU WANT FOR YOUR DOG? 21

CHAPTER 3: BOOTCAMP 27

    HOUSE-TRAINING 28
    THE ALPHA 32
    FOLLOW THE LEADER 35

CHAPTER 4: TRUE DISCIPLINE 39

    DISCIPLINE AS THE OWNER 40
    IS YOUR DOG DISCIPLINED? 42
    IF NOT DISCIPLINE, WHAT ELSE? 44

CHAPTER 5: ADVANCED TRAINING 49

    CLICKER TRAINING 50
    PLAY TIME 52
    STAY! 55
    WHAT ABOUT THE REST? 56

CHAPTER 6: A BRIEF LOOK AT PROFESSIONAL TRAINING 59

    WHAT LEVELS ARE THERE? 60
    WHERE TO GET A SERVICE DOG 65
    THE LAW 66

CHAPTER 7: TAKING CARE OF YOUR FRIEND 69

    YOUR DOG, YOUR RESPONSIBILITY 70
    DIET AND GROOMING 73

Possible Conditions and Afflictions 76
Emotional and Psychological Health 77

Conclusion **79**

References **81**

Introduction

So, you want to train your dog? Well, rest assured, this book will not just help you train your dog, it will also broaden your knowledge surrounding the canine species as a whole. Expanding your knowledge will be a good thing for your pet; you will learn new things alongside your dog, which will help your friendship in the future.

What most people do not realize when they allow a dog into their home is that ultimately, it is, indeed, an animal. Domesticated animals need guidance, and in order for you to take responsibility for that guidance, you need to understand how to provide it. While reading this book, you will be learning many things, or perhaps just rehashing what you already know, ensuring you are on the right track. Let me tell you a story from my younger days, which will help you understand the reasoning behind this book and be more confident in its content.

I have two stepbrothers, one of them being the youngest between all of the siblings. Many years ago, he brought home a puppy that his mother had bought him– to this day I have no idea what breed it was supposed to be. All I know is somewhere in there was part of a Jack Russell Terrier.

To make things easier, we will refer to him as Chase throughout this book.

This is not the first time I had been around a dog, as my father, living on the other side of the country, whom I often visited, had a purebred Pitbull. It did not take me long to realize that for some reason, every time I'd come into contact with a dog, they would always have this strange interest in me. Every owner, and I do mean every owner, of a dog that I have met has told me that their pet will act differently around me, however, not in a disagreeable manner.

The dogs I have met through the years would always enjoy my company, and even this terrifyingly large black Pitbull my father had would come to sit right next to me while I played games. As he practically towered over me while we sat on the floor together, he would respectfully demand my attention. I started to grow intrigued with this newfound power of mine (I was about nine or ten so… give me a break), and I wanted to harness it to the fullest.

I would observe every dog I met, their mannerisms, and their behavior, and then try to command them so they may carry out my will. Well, it didn't always work, as to be expected, and I was quite disappointed. However, just when I started giving up on my newfound power, I started to realize something. Why did some dogs respond to my will and carry it out with such clear intent and accuracy? Why did other dogs ignore me and just simply demand more attention from me until I told them to go away? …Discipline.

Discipline was the answer to my question, as to why not all dogs I meet will listen to me. Well, of course, that's not the only reason, but to my young and naive mind, this could have been the only reason. Make no mistake, this is correct, however, not a complete and mature solution.

But I digress. This new addition to our family, this small and helpless puppy, was no exception to my power, as he was young and ready to be molded by my newly discovered revelation. Unfortunately for him, I moved in with my father for a change of scenery just as he started to get bigger, so I could not train him quite as I wanted, but he wasn't even mine to begin with, so I had no right in the first place.

Nevertheless, I started to notice the severe lack of discipline this dog had developed every time I visited my mother. I concluded that my stepbrother did not really care that much for the dog, and as such, he did not pay attention to the actions it took, and the dog was barely toilet-trained. No one in the house could get the dog to listen to them, however, it was at this point when they noticed that the dog would always be well behaved when he is around me.

I took upon myself the responsibility of training Chase with what little time I had there without anyone realizing. This was not just about teaching him discipline; it was about forming a bond, and we did. He would sleep on the bed next to me, and when I did not want to be disturbed, he would know, because when someone came into my room he would growl at them until they left. He would even know when I was comfortable around someone or not, as he would either allow them near me or would growl at them should they get close to me.

This goes both ways, as I would always protect him should he come looking for asylum from the new bigger dogs.

To this day, my little friend and I get along, even though he has aged, and I do not see him that often anymore. However, every time I do see him, he gets excited beyond his age, and so do I, as we have an unspoken respect for each other. A bond we formed through mutual understanding.

In this book, I will be going over what I have discovered at the tender age of ten, and how I have improved on those discoveries. Learning how to train your dog is not just a chore for you to make sure is done right. It is a ritual you and your dog will go through together, as to achieve a fulfilling and respectable friendship.

There are many methods of training, many things to understand, and many things to learn. In this book, we will not only be looking at training methods used by professionals, but also the basics of forming a good relationship with your dog that will be rewarding for both of you.

Before we get into that, we will be taking a look at the history of the canine as a species, so that we may better understand why they behave the way they do, why certain methods are more effective than others, and why we have dogs as companions in the first place.

So, if you do have a dog already, have them sit next to you as you read through this together. If you do not have one yet and wish to get one, sit back and relax, as this book will further cement your decision of getting one, and make sure you are prepared for the responsibility.

Chapter 1:

When it All Began

The Canine Species is a species we humans have grown close to in the years of our existence together. Dogs and humans have formed something akin to a symbiotic relationship– but of course, not all humans.

Some people sit with their furry friends alone, but together, both needing a friend and someone to rely on. Then, others just want a dog, a friendly animal to have around the house they know is domesticated enough that it won't destroy everything, or attack their friends and family. Many other people might see dogs as simple creatures, a hairy animal which carries disease and parasites, and wonder why they should invite one into their home. There are dogs giving their lives for their nations, in service to the local police force, or to an army. Dogs can create warmth in a family who needs it, and friendship to a child who doesn't have it.

Unfortunately, as I have mentioned, not all humans see dogs as friends. This results in dogs being tragically mistreated, harmed, and even killed for no good reason at all. This is the tragic side of truth between dogs and humans. Luckily, there has been a major increase in the number of people who now believe dogs are significantly more than what humans deserve, as dogs doing good around the world spread over social media forums like wildfire.

Where did all this begin? Or rather, when? How did our relationship with dogs reach a point where we can feel, justifyingly so, more empathy towards them than we do towards certain humans?

It all began with the big brother to all dogs, the Wolf.

The Evolution of the Canine Species

Understanding what your doggy friend is, or trying to understand where this animal came from before you get one, is the key to training it. We will be discussing specific mannerisms in some of the later chapters, so let's learn why these mannerisms exist, and how we should interpret them to better the relationship between dogs and humans.

Way back, and I mean really long ago, like millennia ago... existed one of the most vicious, ferocious mammals still known to us today, the Gray Wolf. This was, quite simply put, an apex predator in certain regions of our small world. A fearsome opponent for any lone-dwelling human, and even more so in packs. In the early days of humanity, we adopted a similar social dynamic as wolves... Was this because we saw them do it first? Regardless of the reason, a small group of humans is triumphantly more successful in surviving the harsh world than a loner, with exceptions of course.

Nonetheless, the wolves had the exact same idea. Imagine placing yourself right outside a wolf pack, observing them without them noticing you. It would become apparent to you that wolves are not as ferocious as they might seem. Yes, they will hunt and kill for food, as well as have their internal skirmishes, but protruding from this violence, is a well-thought-out logical pack, and this is thanks to the pack dynamic.

Usually the average wolf pack will range between three to around seven per pack, but this is just an estimate, as some packs may grow to about 36 wolves. These wolves will select an alpha male and alpha female for the pack to lead. Then, either the alpha male or alpha female may be chosen as the leader to them, beginning the graceful harmony of survival for the pack.

Beta wolves are chosen next, through the same selection process of who is stronger, faster, and wins the fight, be it male or female. The betas are there in case the alphas die, in which case they will fill the power vacuum left. The betas will challenge the alphas to make sure they are still capable of protecting the pack, and should they not be, they will be replaced.

At the bottom of the ranks for this harmonious system, is the omega wolf. The omega will usually be the weakest of the wolves and receives most of the aggressive backlash from all others, which may result in the omega eventually leaving the pack as a lone wolf. However, the omega is important to the pack as much as the others, as the omega will usually be the one to instigate playtime between the wolves, relieving tensions and boosting morale.

This system that they developed worked well, as it protected the group. The alphas are not just the strongest to protect the group, but they also make sure the group doesn't tear itself apart, just as they make sure the young are fed before the others and not killed. The wolves display patterns in behavior that discerns one from the other, which will also be discussed in the later chapters, as it affects the relationship you and your dog might have.

With all of these inner-workings, their territory is easy to manage. A pack can rule over their land, which may easily stretch for miles because they are a pack, and they function as one.

So how did this system, this harmonious collaboration between wolves, evolve into the relationship between dog and human? Well, unfortunately, there is mostly speculation as to how it started. Most likely, early humans started caring for abandoned wolf pups, discovering the benefits of hunting and surviving together. The best we can narrow it down to is tens of thousands of years ago. The evidence found in China, Mongolia, and Europe shows that domesticated dogs started showing up in these regions around that time, give or take a few years.

The gray wolf was not the only canine species back in the day, just the evolutionary ancestor. Through time, we now have other wolves, foxes, African wild dogs, the Dhole, and many others.

Through breeding and diversifying with wolves and other canine species, we now have around 360 breeds, and that's only the officially recognized ones. This doesn't even include experimental breeds and mixed breeds.

These breeds have been shaped by humans, breeding dogs for specific purposes, identifying and using certain attributes to determine which breeds are best suited for what purpose. This is, in a sense, very tragic, as there have been many failures resulting in genetic deformities, with some of these deformities being popularized for personal preference and admiration.

When we look at the domestication process of any animal, it can get quite intricate, especially when we talk about wild animals. Wolves can be domesticated, however, looking back to ancient times, there are records of humans eradicating wolves rather than trying to domesticate them. This does make sense, if you think about it, as wolves are rather ferocious when it comes to feeding the pack, and the amount of food required is about one deer per ten wolves. So, it wouldn't really make sense to hunt with wolves at that point in time—at least not with wild and untrained ones.

There are some people who believe that at the end of the day, we never even domesticated dogs, but rather the exact opposite, that they domesticated us. As I mentioned previously, the possibility of humans domesticating wolves most likely started with someone caring for a lost pup. However, that is just one side of the coin ; what if the wolf came to him?

The records of humans eradicating wolves rather than keeping them alive weigh staggeringly in the former's favor, so what is the likelihood that we actually approached them first? In Europe, humans ordered the killing of wolves centuries ago, even offering bounties per wolf. In some regions, they burned down entire forests to rid them of this intimidating predator. In North America, the wolf population was hunted almost to extinction by the beginning of the 20th century.

By this time, however, we had already been living with dogs in our houses, albeit most of them stayed outside in their little dog houses. What if, in the end, the wolves did approach us instead? They might have realized they would be wiped out if they didn't act more friendly and docile towards humans, and change their way of life. This resulted in one of the most important changes that made it possible for us to train them.

These friendly wolves started to pass their genes onto the next generation and so forth, resulting in communication between humans and wolves becoming more streamlined, as the mannerisms exhibited by the wolves became much more pronounced. They started wagging their tails around, turning their heads sideways, and flapping their ears. Their mental state changed as well. They started to learn how to interpret our voiced commands and physical gestures, which we will discuss later on when we take an in-depth look at gestures during training.

The takeaway here is that dogs are now much more intelligent than they used to be. Just as our intellects have evolved, so have theirs. Their knowledge of humans has increased tremendously, making training them much easier.

For good or for bad, we have shaped the canine species into what it is today.

The Historical Impact of the Canine Species

Now let's jump a bit forward in time to when dogs started getting domesticated. We started realizing that dogs are more intelligent than we originally thought, and can, therefore, be of considerably more use to us if trained properly.

Back in ancient times, dogs were used for protection and in the form of weapons on the human battlefield. As far back as 600 B.C., there are records of dogs being used when the Lydian king sent them out to break up the enemy formations on the field. This sad yet crucial historical fact helped shape the relationship between man and dog, as they developed a stronger bond.

Jumping forward again, we arrive at WWI. At this point in time, we have developed a much more loving relationship with our dogs, as we have endured the struggles of survival together. We have learned how to work together, to live together, and be a family together; now the third biggest war the world has seen will disrupt the friendship between humans and dogs.

At first, dogs were simply being used as mascots to boost unit morale in this time of great war, and soon proved themselves worthy as more than just a mascot, but also as a brother in arms. There was a dog in the American 102nd infantry unit known as Stubby. Stubby saved soldiers by being a type of early warning unit for the infantry against enemy infantry, artillery, and even gas attacks. Stubby was wounded at one point, however, he survived and joined the fight again, and was promoted to Sargent after doing so well.

This was simply the start, and WWI started to branch out into a whole new type of war. More dogs were employed to help fellow engineers make sure communications weren't interrupted by laying cable. Other dogs were being used to run messages that were part of the crucial communications network as they were smaller, faster, and more agile than normal infantry. Thanks to their trustworthy and reliable nature, training the dogs properly made them into heroes to some on the battlefield.

After this tragic time, the militaries of the world started using dogs more, realizing their potential even further when proper training is given, and trust between soldier and dog was encouraged.

Regrettably, a few years later, World War II came to be, and the dogs were recruited again, providing services similar to WWII, receiving new positions as well. This began with the first organized deployment of dogs throughout the battlefield. Brattain opened their first dog training school for military application, from which nearly 76, 000 graduated by 1944.

These dogs were deployed in many units, such as the paratroops, guards, minefield detection, and communications, some even donning gas masks when on the front lines. The Soviets adopted a more controversial use for the dogs, strapping them with magnetic mines on their backs and training them to scamper underneath tanks, detonating the mine, and disabling the tank along with gruesomely killing the dog. The Russians used this method intensively for a while. However, some dogs would become terrified by the amount of gunfire surrounding them, causing them to run back to their handlers in the trenches, often detonating the mine.

There were many dogs in WWII recognized as heroes, dogs like "Chips'. He was the most decorated dog in WWII, traveling between Germany, Africa, Sicily, and France. Chips started earning his stripes amongst the soldiers, and even played a role in capturing 10 enemy soldiers inside a machine gun nest. Chips was honored with a Purple Heart, Silver Wings, and Distinguished Service Cross.

A small little Yorkshire Terrier known as "Smoky" took part in quite a few combat missions and survived around 150 air raids. She was found abandoned in a foxhole on the field and was adopted and served as an early warning against artillery and enemy troops. She boosted morale and famously kept engineers and infantry safe by running a communications cable through a pipe for them, resulting in no extra construction needed. "Nemo" was known in the Vietnam War for defending against a surprise VietCong guerilla attack. Nemo protected the handler until reinforcements arrived.

Dogs have helped us in these tragic and trying times, and as such, we have come to understand that dogs deserve more than what we have provided for them. In these modern times, we unfortunately still face the truth of war, and our canine friends are still standing right next to us. A dog known as "Bak" gave his life in Afghanistan when he and his handler came under fire while searching for explosives. He detected a total of six major improvised explosive devices, and as a result, saved many lives.

When we look back, we realize how the relationship between humans and dogs has evolved into something different than what it was in the past. We now understand more about each other and have changed the way we handle and train dogs to be functioning members of our society. It is almost strange to think about how long we have been collaborating in this world, surviving and fighting together.

How This Has Affected Dog Training

So, right at this moment, you might be a bit confused as to why I have given you a brief look into the history of our most tragic moments as a human race. However you may look at it, training your dog today is most certainly not going to be the same as training your dog centuries ago—and why is that? Well, there are several answers to that, but the most prominent is our relationships between each other and our dogs. We don't look at our dogs as mere tools for survival anymore; we look at them and see our affectionate furry friends. Unfortunately, there are drawbacks to this mentality in specific situations.

Through everything we have learned, we don't just see dogs; we see friends, and even a part of the family, which is in some respects true, but this does not mean that a dog is not still an animal. They need guidance and discipline. Who else can give that but the owner? This is a responsibility that every owner must realize when looking into getting a dog, be it as a friend, hunting partner, protector, and even as a service dog.

When humans first started training their dogs, they did not necessarily know or understand how intelligent dogs were, and did not know their limits, resulting in either an injured dog or inadequate training. Training hundreds of years ago was simple. The dog did not have to account for much; it had to either keep their owner safe or help them hunt, maybe guard a specific property and alert their owner of an intruder, or simply be a friendly pet in order to lift the spirits of children during difficult times.

This slowly progressed into more detailed training, thus requiring attention to specific details such as the breed of the dog, and asking questions about what certain breeds do best? What are its weaknesses? What service would you like the dog to provide in exchange for you feeding it and taking care of it? Questions like this started arising, and so the number of breeds available increased with the demand.

When the men in WWI had dogs on military grounds, the dogs needed to be disciplined and well-trained to avoid any disruptions amongst the military personnel and tactics. This was taken even further when they started to use the dogs in the field. Dogs earned their ranks in WWII when, as we learned, training was now an official part of the armies of the world. They were trained professionally, and not just by an infantryman who had an affinity towards picking up strays. They were being provided with the best available attention at that point in time.

With all these lessons we have learned through time, through our hardships side by side with wolves and eventually dogs, there are two major points we must consider when dealing with dogs:

Discipline and Domestication.

When we look at those two words, we might think, wow OK, aren't those the basic principles of having a dog? Well, yes, that is exactly correct. The problem comes in when people do not know how to discipline their dogs, and the dogs break free from domestication. As we have discussed our history between dogs and humans, there is one thing that lays frighteningly apparent: dogs were once wolves, and some of those traits may arise if not properly regulated.

This is where discipline comes in. We have developed this sense of safety around dogs, which I understand, however, this does not mean we should not discipline our dogs. How else will they know how to distinguish between what is allowed, and what is not?

Just because dogs have been domesticated in general, does not mean they can not go back into the wild and become the apex predator they once were. Through years of trial and error, dog training has reached a point where it is easy enough to train your dog by yourself, with techniques specifically designed to work best on whichever breed you wish to bring into your home. Even just teaching the basics does not require that much skill, only a shred of patience.

So here we are with our pets, or maybe you have not gotten one yet and want to prepare yourself for the coming responsibility. Either way, I wish I could get another dog, but unfortunately, I do not have space or the grounds in order to sustain another. Speaking of which, we need to take a look at how to prepare yourself, your house, and your yard for training your dog.

Chapter 2:

Before Getting a Dog

Preparation before getting a dog might sound like a strange topic to discuss, however, do not be too quick to dismiss the idea that preparation is key in any situation.

Don't believe me? Let me tell you a story then...

I mentioned my father's purebred pitbull, but what I did not mention is the fact that he also had two other dogs, both being Jack Russell Terriers. At this point in time the pitbull was quite young, and as a matter of fact, so was I. I do, however, remember one thing: my father went everywhere with one of the Jack Russells, who we'll call Jack. Jack was an aggressive little monster to be honest, not towards family and friends at least, but only towards strangers.

This is one of the reasons my father took him on his business trips. Jack mostly listened to him, not solely, but he was the only one able to halt any misbehavior. My father worked on many construction sites and had to drive all over the place, taking Jack with him for the ride. He would tell me stories about some men being afraid of walking near his truck because of Jack barking maniacally at anyone who approached the vehicle, jumping up against the window with his slobber smearing over it, daring them to open the door. I've seen this dog in action before, and he really did look terrifyingly crazy.

I remember that Jack was not fond of other animals, except the ones he already knew, and had no interest in making new friends. This was apparent when I witnessed his response to the neighbors' dogs for the first time. They came to say hello with their two German Shepherds in tow, and thus, the little maniac went wild, barking and jumping up against the fence. They forgot about the little monster, apologized, and came back after taking their dogs back home. He tolerated them by themselves, since father was around to scold him when he tried to act up.

Unfortunately, due to lack of upkeep and repairs to the fence between us and the neighbors, little Jack escaped into their yard one night. Well, let me just say we all suffered a tragic loss that night.

This story is an unfortunate one, nonetheless, it has more than one key lesson hidden in the text... were you able to identify them? If not, there's no need to worry. I will be going over them as we proceed through this chapter of discussing how to prepare for owning a dog, and ultimately deciding what type of training you would like to provide your pet.

What is Needed

The first thing we think about when we want to get a dog is usually the breed. This is a good first step, however, it all depends on where you will be getting your new dog from. Many people feel it is better to adopt one or more from the local dog shelter, and this is indeed a great option. When adopting a new dog, there are a few things to consider before going to the shelter and just walking out, dog in hand.

There may be more than one shelter in your area, and usually, these shelters don't have the necessary infrastructure to process all the adoption applications quickly, and this means you might have to be a bit more forbearing than originally planned. Adopting from a shelter is encouraged, and if you don't have a specific breed in mind, this is the best option for both you and the dog.

The other option you have is going to a licensed dog breeder. These are a bit more controversial depending on your area, and also are a bit more difficult to find. Breeders usually specialize in a specific pure breed and might end up being a bit more expensive, so if you have a specific breed in mind, this might be your best option. Whether you are going to the local dog shelter or a well-known breeder, you will need one thing:

The correct mentality.

Getting a new dog comes with a big responsibility. Who will be taking care of the dog's basic needs? Who will make sure the dog is healthy? Are there any other animals in the surrounding area or in the same house? All of these things need to be considered, and you need to be mentally prepared for this as well. This was one of the mistakes made when taking care of Jack, that not everyone in the family really knew what their role was when taking care of the dogs, but this was not one of the reasons things ended up as they did.

If you will be the only one responsible for the dog, that's great, since it makes managing responsibility easier, however, it might lead to forgetting or neglecting your responsibility. In this case, it might be better to write down a list of daily tasks that you must perform to ensure the health and safety of your new friend. If you share a home or apartment with other people, confirm with them first if they will be comfortable with a dog around them, which is paramount as one of them might be allergic and won't be able to tolerate having a dog.

Something else to prepare for when you are the only one caring for the dog is where the dog will be kept when you are not there, and making sure you have emergency contacts set up in case something should happen and you cannot go home to feed your dog. If the dog is going to be a new member of your family, even better! This way your pet will never be bored and responsibilities can be divided equally.

Having covered all of that, you need to remember that the dog will be dependent on you, and you must be sure you are ready for the responsibility.

Moving along, we also need to cover what type of purchases you will need to make in order for you to keep your new friend happy. This will all depend on the environment in which the dog will be raised, and of course what age it will be. Should you adopt from a shelter, chances are, your furry friend won't be a pup.

In this case, remember to give your dog some time to adjust to its new environment, and make sure it is comfortable and not too stressed out. Basic products to keep in mind will be things like toys, food, bowls for food and water, bedding, blankets if the region tends to be cold, a dog house if applicable, and of course a leash, collar, and tag. Now that I think about it, Jack never really had a lot of toys to play with.

Puppies are usually around 8 weeks old when they leave their litter, so when getting your new friend from a breeder, this is the likely age it will be. In this case, you will have to get the same items as mentioned previously, however, when considering a leash, the harness option is usually the most fitting solution given the puppies' small body. Another item to consider beforehand is proper dog shampoo, should the day come that your friend has a messy play date in some mud.

When talking about your new pet, we can't avoid the discussion surrounding a proper vet. Should your new friend become sick or injured, it will be your responsibility to make sure he or she is taken to someone who can provide proper diagnosis and treatment. You don't want to scatter and stumble when an injury does occur, so it's better to do some research towards finding a trustworthy vet located close to you. Insurance can also be an option, as it helps a lot should something drastic happen, however not everyone feels that it's necessary.

Speak With Your Family First

This is an important one, considering none of us knew my stepbrother would be bringing a dog home. His father was taken by surprise, but did not really have a choice at that point, seeing as the puppy was already there. This will also help you go over safety measures for you, your family, and the new furry member.

First, at least discuss with your family if they want a dog, and the rules involved in getting a dog, such as responsibility-sharing. Make sure you all understand how to avoid injuring your new friend, and though this might sound a bit jarring, you'd be surprised by how many people do not understand the limits when playing with a puppy or dog.

I believe the puppy my stepbrother brought in was a victim of poor planning. No one knew how to train Chase, and no one really paid attention to him enough, except my stepbrother and me. This was apparent in the way he responded to their commands or calls, however, it did get better later on, as he got older.

This was a major problem when dealing with Jack as well, being that he was very sensitive and did not like certain things, causing him to act unnecessarily aggressively. If proper boundaries were put in place and he was taught not to act out, the events of that night could have been avoided. Even if just the right amount of time was spent with him to make sure his physiological needs were met, it could've been avoided as well.

Let's talk about one of the main reasons things ended up as they did, my hope being that you do not make the same mistakes we did.

Preparing Your Home

Now, this might be different depending on the weather conditions in your region and whether or not your pet will be staying with you in an apartment, a suburban house, or a farm. A good baseline is comparing your comfort to your dogs. If you are cold, your dog most likely is as well, and the same goes with warmth. The weather is not the only thing you should prepare for though, as there are many things to keep an eye out for when you first bring a dog home, as well as things to check up on in the future.

Let's start with your interior, as this will be the center of your new friend's world.

Something to keep in mind is the breed of your dog, as some breeds tend to have certain mannerisms that others do not. Like most Jack Russell Terriers, Jack had an affinity to sniff out shoes and completely obliterate them when younger. This can happen with many breeds, as it's a natural way to relieve stress. If you don't want your shoes destroyed, make sure to keep them in places your dog won't be able to reach.

Take a look around your house and decide on areas where the dog will not be allowed to be. It is best to make preparations for this beforehand by partitioning these parts using dividers. This will also help with training your pet later on, to a point where dividers won't be needed. If you are comfortable with your pet running around the whole house, then no worries. Jack had free-roaming privileges in my father's house, except for the kitchen, and this was enforced through dividers he made and placed there when Jack was still young. In contrast, the puppy my stepbrother brought home goes around the house jumping on beds and running all over the property with no restrictions.

I'm not saying that it's a bad thing, but just keep in mind that if no physical restrictions are in place when your dog is young, it will be more difficult to train your dog in the future, should you decide to do so.

Now that you have decided where your dog will be allowed access and where not, take a look at your space. Will your dog be sleeping in the same room as you? On the bed, or in its own bed? Either way, be sure to plan ahead so that when you bring the dog in, you can take them directly to "their space". This will help get them comfortable and ease into the new environment. If you have coffee tables or anything like that around, keep in mind the size of the breed you want, because, if not properly trained, your pet might steal that sandwich off the lower-level table. Related to furniture is breakables as well, if you have any lone standing vases or small statues, they might get knocked over when your little friend gets excited.

Toilet-training will depend on your house as well. If you have a big yard, then it will be quite obvious where the business will go down. In this case, you must plan for access to that area as well, will a doggy door work for you? Will you be opening and closing the door for your dog, or will your friend spend most of its time outside?

Speaking about outside, what do you think could be a problem in your property? Save for the obvious hole in the fence, but there might be other things that can pose a danger. Some breeds like to dig, and I have seen many dogs dig their way out underneath a fence. The easiest way this can be avoided is by inspecting your property at least twice a week for any holes that might have been dug while you were otherwise occupied. Another telltale sign is when your dog is covered in soil, you will immediately notice the extra soil in your house and all over their paws, nose, and fur.

While you are outside, pay attention to any holes that might appear in your fencing. If you stay on a farm, this will obviously be impossible, and the dog will also be more used to big open spaces, so it shouldn't be an issue. Lastly, many people forget to think about poisonous substances they use to deter insects and unwanted plants, and when doing some research you will find there are better options out there that do not affect your dogs' health.

So, having covered your preparation for getting a dog, let's get to the good stuff: the training. There are a few things to cover for you to understand your dog a little better, so let's get to it, shall we?

What Training Do You Want for Your Dog?

The biggest reason behind the aggression of old Jack was protection. In a way, my father taught him to be rather aggressive. It worked, as he was very protective of my father when he went on his trips, however, in the end, it backfired. He never took the time to train Jack on when to be aggressive and when not to be. He also never enforced the proper commands in order for Jack to understand when to stop.

What type of training are you looking to reinforce with your new friend? As an example, I will use Chase. I knew exactly what type of response I wanted from the dog when I said certain things. I never really minded when he jumped on my bed, so long as he was clean, and he knew this. I made sure he understood that if he was covered in mud he may not jump on the bed. Of course, it didn't work all the time, as sometimes dogs just get very excited and forget, especially since I did not stay there permanently, so I never committed the right amount of time to the training.

When I walked into my room, I would snap my finger over the bed so he would jump up, he would wag his tail and I'd follow by tapping on my chest while standing next to the bed, signaling that he may jump up against me for some well-deserved petting, puppy talk, and attention. This worked very well as I can simply snap my finger over a chair, table or bed and he would jump up, if there is no snap, he knew he can't jump up.

So let's take a minute and think about what you want your dog to understand at the end of a training period. Do you want your friend to be able to understand some gestures? Vocal commands? Or maybe you just want your dog to know the basics and don't intend to enforce advanced discipline, which is also fine, in fact, it's just much more simple. In the end, it doesn't matter all that much, but what does matter is the bond created between you and your dog. While training, a bond can get much stronger as trust becomes a big part of your relationship, especially in a more professional environment.

Thinking ahead will help greatly, as you can start enforcing the rules for your training as soon as possible, and having a structured plan can work wonders. You can start training your new friend the minute you bring him or her home, however, it is best to have them settle in first for a day or so. A training schedule may include basic toilet-training, to simply sit and follow commands, teaching them their name, or reinforcing a response to a specific sound like a whistle or clap/snap.

Before training starts, let's quickly take a look at some basic mannerisms some dogs and breeds might exhibit so you can understand your dog's feelings better. After all, you can't expect your new friend to follow your commands if you can't even understand their basic feelings, right?

Biting - Puppies usually nip and bite a lot, as this is their basic form of communication, and it also helps stimulate the development of their teeth. Other reasons for biting when your dog is a bit older might be linked to anxiety, stress, fear, or simple aggression. It is best to stop this type of behavior if there is no immediate reason for it to be happening, and ensure your dog they are safe by providing an innocuous and wholesome environment. Should this behavior persist, it would be best to consult a professional dog trainer.

Squinting/Intense staring/Leaning against you - Dog owners know this look; it might only show up a bit later when your dog is no longer a puppy. They give you this squinting, judgmental look as if you just did something very wrong… well, you did. You receive this look when you don't give your friend enough attention! Maybe you have been a bit busy with work or just preoccupied, but either way, this look usually means they are awaiting attention of which you have been depriving them… so then they judge you for it. Not to worry though, it's not permanent. Just give your friend a little love and attention, and they will be happy again. When they lean against you it's not necessarily judgmental, they just want some attention!

Sitting between your legs/on your feet - When your dog does this, they usually feel unsafe or threatened, so use this opportunity to build trust with your pet by providing some comfort. You can take a look around as well, as something may have startled them.

Digging - This is normal behavior for a dog and is nothing to be alarmed about, however, you might want to make sure you address this behavior at a young age so as to avoid damage to your property in the future.

Tongue out/Floppy ears - This is a good thing, meaning that your friend is happy and relaxed; nothing can kill their vibe right now.

Ears back and snarling/Teeth out/Low growl - Being quite obvious, your dog is most likely warning you or something/someone else not to touch them, and this is a show of aggression. When training, be sure to show dominance in order to avoid this behavior towards you, however, we will discuss this in the next chapter.

Erratic barking - When your dog is jumping around wagging their tail, barking erratically, with the pitch of the bark rising and lowering, they are most likely ready to play and can't contain their excitement. Take this time to play with them at least a little bit, and it will reinforce your bond.

Licking - Also quite an obvious one, if your dog licks you they are showing submissive behavior and affection. Some people find it a bit repulsive, which is understandable, and in this case, it is better to discourage such behavior from a young age.

Howling - When your dog is howling, it's most likely due to them hearing a high pitched sound that you might not be able to hear yourself. This is normal behavior, although it can be a bit annoying at night.

Head tilt - this is one of the more adorable things your dog might do. When this happens they are most likely trying to adjust their hearing due to an interesting sound, or just out of curiosity!

Now that you understand your dog a bit better, there are more mannerisms to look out for, however, these are the basic ones that most breeds exhibit. Something else to keep in mind is that every dog is different! Your friend might do something other dogs do not usually bother doing, and that's normal, just remember to handle the behavior in a constructive manner.

Your house is prepared inside out for your new friend, you've settled on a breed, you know what type of relationship you want with your dog, and what training you would like to reinforce with your dog, so let's start with the basic training every furry best friend needs in order to facilitate a healthy relationship.

Chapter 3:

Bootcamp

Have you ever walked into a vet and seen the different temperaments and levels of discipline the animals have? When I traveled in a different country, I was truly astonished by the difference in behavior the dogs had compared to where I came from. There were a lot of strays in this country, however, they were so well-behaved and friendly, that I wanted to take every single one I met home! We had to go to a vet with a friend we made there, and as we sat in the waiting room, I was observing everything around me.

There was a big black dog lying in front of its master, an old man with a stern look on his face. The dog seemed curious as to what was going on around him, so I lowered my voice as an attempt to obtain this beautiful beast's attention.The dog took notice and slowly stood up, he sat straight and looked up at his master, looked at me, and looked up at his master again. The old man noticed what I was trying to do, he looked down at his friend and so subtly gave a nod to him as if he approved of what was about to transpire. The dog stood up and walked towards me while wagging his tail, ever so gently.

Reverence washed over me as the dog sat down in front of me and placed his head gently on my lap, almost as if he was confirming with me if this is okay. I rubbed his back and patted his head for almost ten minutes as he just sat there and smiled. The old man did not mind at all as he sat there and simply smiled. We did not speak the same language, but I understood one thing, that these two have been together as friends for a long time. As the old man's name was called, he made a sound with his mouth which I'm not exactly sure how to explain, but the dog, however, understood. He followed his master all the way down the hall and disappeared through one of the doors.

Unfortunately, I did not see them again, as my friend came back from dropping off his cat, and off we went. To this day, I can still remember the look on the old man's face and the dog's face, both fully aware of what the other was thinking, and knew they trusted each other, and respected each other. I could feel compassion this man had for his furry friend as they both passed me by, and as the dog left my side to follow his master, I could tell he was proud to be this man's protector.

Not everyone desires this level of training, respect, pride, trust, friendship, or discipline from their pets, and that is completely understandable. Not everyone has the time to make sure it is on that level in the first place, as some people just simply want a dog to be in their lives. That is fine as well, however, even if you just want a basic relationship with your dog, you must teach them the basics. Otherwise, you might get annoyed or frustrated with their behavior, resulting in both being unhappy.

Let's look at the basic training every dog needs.

House-Training

First, did you just bring a new puppy into your home? Or did you adopt an older dog from a nearby shelter? Depending on your answer, toilet-training, or rather, house-training, will be different.

A new puppy can take a while to house-train. On average, it's usually between four and six months. If you adopted an older dog, the chance that they are already house-trained is very high, almost a given. They will, however, require a refresher course; you just brought them into a whole new environment after all. There are two different ways of reinforcing your dog's behavior: positive reinforcement and negative reinforcement. This will vary between what you are trying to teach your dog, however, the best is usually positive.

Positive reinforcement is simply reward-based training where you reward your friend with either snacks or petting when the task is accomplished successfully. This is the preferred method, as it builds a stronger relationship between you and your dog, making sure there is no room for resentment later on. This is the best option especially when house-training a new puppy, as you are laying down the basic foundation for the type of relationship you will have—a strict and almost cold one, or a more warm and compassionate one. There are, of course, situations that require a negative response, but more on that later.

When training a puppy, it is important to keep an eye out for where they are heading. You might be busy doing something while observing them from the corner of your eye, but follow them if they disappear and make sure they don't have bathroom plans, otherwise, you might end up with a small puddle right around the corner, or worse.

Things to look out for when you suspect your puppy might be wanting to go is: pacing or circling around the same area, sniffing on the ground with intent, whining or barking, heading towards where you usually take them when you go outside, or starting to squat over the ground. When this happens, do not yell at them or clap, that will scare them, and in the end, they might associate the very act of going to the toilet with punishment. Try to get their attention in a positive manner, make them excited as if you are going to give them a treat, and this will more than likely distract them enough so you can either pick them up or get them to follow you outside.

It's important to take your dog outside regularly, which will minimize inside accidents from happening, and on the other hand, provide you with the opportunity to praise them with attention or a snack when they do what they are supposed to, where they are supposed to. Keep in mind that it is better to stay with your dog outside for a few minutes every time you take them out, so you can use this opportunity to play with them a bit and build your friendship, establish boundaries (we will discuss this later), and manage your bond.

You will not want to leave your new puppy outside on its own when just starting out, as there are many exciting things in a yard for them. New sights, smells, and sounds will be exciting to them, and he or she might not think about getting down to business right away. You will have to make peace with the fact that, for the first few times you go out with them, you will have to stay a bit longer.

You don't want to stay outside forever though. you might start to get annoyed with your dog, and they will feel your frustration. Simply take your puppy back in after a few minutes if they don't seem to be interested in doing their business just yet. After a while, you will get used to the routine your puppy has, and then shape it into what you desire.

In a few weeks time, your friend will get used to the idea of getting praised when they do their business outside, this will result in proper toilet-training. Keep in mind that after a few weeks, they will be getting used to it, but that doesn't mean accidents don't happen. It can take a few months for your friend to get completely used to the idea of 'outside = good' and 'inside = bad'.

While going out, try to use the same route and exit every time, placing them on the same spot as well. This will further reinforce where to go and how to get there, making sure it's the first place they think of when getting the urge to go potty. Unfortunately, this means you will have to get up during the night as well to take them out. If you are able to leave your door open a bit during the night it will help, otherwise, the installation of a doggy door will help. Just be sure to show your dog how it works after they have learned the whole 'outside good, inside bad' concept.

This can work with windows as well. I used to keep my window open when staying with my mother, I showed this to Chase so he could understand if he jumped through there, he can get outside quicker than running all the way to the front door. He caught on pretty quickly, and soon enough he would camp out on the corner of my bed, right next to the window, so I guess he enjoyed the view.

So you just stood outside for thirty minutes, your puppy has not done anything but run around and play, you are cold so you take your friend back inside, and 10 minutes later you discover a small puddle on the floor… What do you do now?

Don't try and stick their nose in it and punish them in a negative way. It won't work, they might lose trust in you, as they are still very young and won't even recall what they did wrong. Simply clean the area in a neutral manner and make sure it is cleaned properly to avoid them coming back to the same spot and smelling what they left behind. At a young age, it's better to focus on positive reinforcement. Later on as the dog gets older, they will be able to understand negative reinforcement in a constructive manner.

If after a few months, your dog is still going inside, this might be a medical or psychological problem. Doing their business inside after being shown where it should be done, can be a sign of either stress or loneliness. Either way, it will be best to consult a professional trainer or vet in this case.

Contrastly, instead of getting a puppy, you opted for adoption from a shelter. This usually means house-training will be less of a fuss, however, this is not guaranteed. You don't know what exactly transpired in the past, what mannerisms the dog has learned from previous owners, or while staying in the shelter. Accidents will be minimal, as adult dogs are able to hold it in with more control than puppies.

Take your new friend outside in the mornings and in the evenings before bed, a couple of times during the day will help as well, but it all depends on your living arrangements. You will have to stay outside for a bit with them, and just like with puppies, when you try using positive reinforcement the first few times, they will learn much quicker. You can keep a lookout for the telltale signs that they wish to go as well, like whining, barking, or even scratching at the door.

Keep in mind that your dog is very unsure at the moment. It's a new environment, with new smells and sounds everywhere, and you do not know what happened in the dog's past either, so be as patient as possible.

So your new friend, be it puppy or adult, knows where to do their business and how to get there. Let's talk about something that you can reinforce while providing house-training, which will help with future training and discipline as well.

The Alpha

The one, unmistakable fact for the dogs in my father's house, was that he was the alpha. Remember the part about how the wolves have a functioning hierarchy, with the alpha on top? Then you might also remember that dogs originated from wolves... What does that tell you? You need to establish the alpha in your pack, and you don't want it to be your dog.

Finding the balance between positive and negative reinforcement will help when establishing the alpha. Even just neutral behavior from your side at the right time can mean the difference between a well-mannered pet and a demanding hound.

Starting off, you cannot spoil your dog every opportunity you get, as this will result in very demanding behavior, so be careful not to give too many treats and/or attention when using positive reinforcement. It is not just about what you give and take; it is how you present yourself when doing so. Dogs have a very keen sense of feeling the intent behind what you are doing, or about to do.

When my mother tells Chase that he has to get off the couch, he doesn't bother, because she never commanded him with intent, and if she tried to move him, he would growl at her, after which she would resort to either sitting next to him or calling me if I was home. When she does call me, I would simply look at him and tell him "off", after which he'd immediately comply by jumping off and running towards me, and I would usually give him a light pet for his obedience. Giving your dog a little attention when they listen is important, but not too much, a simple pat on the head and a "good doggy" is fine. This reinforces the idea that if they listen to you, good things happen.

The way you command your dog must have intent behind it. You have to mean what you say, and you have to feel what you say. Doing this when house-training your dog will make sure they grow up understanding that there are consequences behind their actions, and the intent to enforce those consequences behind your words.

Something to remember is that your dog must earn those treats. They have to do their business outside in order to get a treat or petting when your dog wants attention, you can't simply give it to them. They have to complete a form of command before getting attention, something as simple as when I tap on my chest and Chase jumps up, only then is he allowed to get attention.

When you command with intent while training, the dog will automatically pick up on who is the alpha, however, some dogs are more stubborn than others.

Something that will help with establishing the alpha is the pecking order.

I remember a few times that I went over to a friends house, I would sit at the table for lunch, and their dog would come begging for food. Many times I would make eye contact and state with intent "no", a word most dogs recognize. Now most of the time this would work, but some dogs were not taught proper discipline, and in other cases, I am not the alpha, so why should they listen to me? It's not my house or my pack.

When establishing who eats first, you always eat your meal first before providing them theirs. You can do this by taking a bite of your food in front of them and only then, place their bowl on the ground, or they can wait until you are completely finished. When giving them snacks, if it's edible to humans, take a bite out of it first before giving it to your dog, this establishes that your dog is not allowed to eat before you do. You can do this in different places around the house and in public as well, it will help enforce the idea that no matter the situation, no matter where or when, you eat first.

Another effective way of making sure you stay the alpha is manipulating playtime with your dog's toys. In order for this to work the best possible way, you will need at least five different toys. These items do not even have to be actual toys; maybe a stick your dog found and chews on, or a ball. Keep two or three of these designated toys around the house or outside during the day, and when night comes, pick up the toys and put them away, making sure your dog sees you do so. Take the toys out the following morning while your dog watches, be sure to rotate the toys daily, and should they find something new to play with. Or, if you buy a new toy, add it to the rotation schedule.

During the day, when playing with your dog, if they are unnecessarily aggressive or refuse to give you one of the designated toys that day, take it and put it away. Don't take it out again until the following day, making sure they have fewer toys to play with for that day. This will ensure your dog understands that you are in charge and should he misbehave, you will punish him, and this is a very good example of negative reinforcement without going too far, causing trauma.

A more subtle way of making sure your dog remembers who the alpha is, is by making them move out of your way every once in a while. You can do this calmly without inciting aggression. Having the intent of causing harm should your dog not move, is enough for your dog to feel dominance coming from you. When Chase sits on my bed or on a couch, I sometimes make a point of not sitting next to him, but rather tell him to move or make him move to the other side, then I sit where he was. Remember, you are the alpha, you sit where you want, you walk where you want, and your dog needs to remember that. You don't have to do this every day, just a few times a week is fine. Even if they are just laying on the floor, don't step over them or around, make them move out of the way so you can pass. There are other methods to reinforce the idea that you are the alpha of the pack, and we will discuss them in later chapters as they fall in nicely with those specific training techniques.

Remember, simply telling your dog to do something louder, is not necessarily saying something with intent, it's just aggression. You have to feel what you are saying, project your intent, and be prepared to act should your dog not respond the way they should.

OK, now you know how to be the alpha, so let's use that to build on the foundation you laid down for your dog's training through positive reinforcement, molding it into something more than just human and dog staying together.

Follow The Leader

You have your basics. In fact, most people do not train their dogs more than what has been discussed, and that's ok, but you want more, don't you? Let's take a look at another few basic things to teach your dog that will make it much easier in the future.

How to sit. A concept which many dogs already understand, the trick comes in to make them sit when you want them to, and this has many applications ranging from reinforcing dominance, to having them complete a command before getting a treat so they do not become spoiled, to simply sitting somewhere and waiting for you to return.

Starting off, you will want to do this in a space your dog is used to by now. This helps them feel comfortable and makes it more likely they will listen, especially when they are still young, as their attention span is quite limited. You will also need to provide your friend with a few breaks in between; just like when we study a new subject and need breaks in between, so do they, otherwise focus will be minimal.

Indoors will be best, as there are fewer distractions and it's an environment that is easier to keep control over. Should you have family or roommates around, inform them about your intentions to make sure they do not introduce any distractions while you are busy. If you like the fresh air and your dog is more used to being outside, try to keep them on a leash or in a controlled space, otherwise, the difficulty of training will go up exponentially, especially if you don't have your dominant act together yet. By this time, you should have a pretty good read on your friend's emotions, and how to identify and interpret certain mannerisms they display. This is important, so when your training session starts, you should be able to tell if they are focused on the task at hand, responding well to your commands, and absorbing what is being taught. After a few minutes, you will start to realize that your dog seems distracted and not as focused as when you started, and that's normal of course, so take a break for a few minutes.

Take this time to stock up on some treats for your friend, as you will need them to keep their attention, and also make sure the environment you choose is the best option. When selecting treats, don't just take anything available in the kitchen, as there are some forms of human food that may be very unhealthy or even poisonous to dogs. In a later chapter, we will take an in-depth look at healthy treats and foods, as well as poisonous or unhealthy things you should watch out for.

Starting off, you will want to capture your friend's full attention. Stand right in front of them; this will, of course, make you the center focal point long enough for you to introduce a seductive treat. Now, if you have been reinforcing proper intent and dominance, they will understand that they can't just take it, although the excitement might get the better of them and they will try, but do not let them. Remember, for your dog to get a treat, they must earn it, so it is enough for them just to notice you have it, that will keep their attention on either you or the treat.

Keeping the treat closed in your hand, hold it in front of their nose and start to slowly move your hand over their nose to the top of the head and finally right at the back of their head, make sure it's close enough so that your dog won't have to jump up to get to your hand. This might take a few tries, but you will notice your dog will try and follow your hand with their nose, and because of the direction your hand is going, they will lower their backside and finally sit. If your friend is not sitting quite completely flat, you can gently push down on their backside, easing them into the sit position.

Sometimes when doing this, your dog will try and walk backward to follow the treat, so make sure there's a wall or fence behind them to limit their movement the first few tries. When your dog finally sits, remember to say the word "sit" with dominant intent and firmness. If your dog does not sit, avoid saying something like "no, sit" or anything similar, you need your dog to associate the word "sit" with the act of sitting and then being either praised or given a treat.

Do this a few times. Every time they sit, give them positive attention or a treat. After a week or so of doing this every day, you can stop giving treats and simply praise them. Of course, every now and then you can still give them a treat, but not too many though. Some dogs may require some physical guidance depending on their personalities. Naturally, some dogs are more docile and obedient, but then you get other dogs who are a bit more energetic. In this case, it would be best to get a leash and harness in order for you to stay in control of the situation, ignore any negative behavior, and positively react to good behavior.

Using the leash, keep them close and in front of you, and you can try the same method discussed above. If this does not work, your friend might need some physical guidance. However, do not hit or spank your dog, and do not force them down. This can hurt your friend, and in the end, the only thing they will learn is fear, which they might react to by either biting or running. Keep in mind, if you have the full intent of dominance behind your posture and words, your dog will pick up on this as well, making the process more streamlined. After a while, you can start moving to different locations and have them sit in different places, further reinforcing this command.

So now your dog knows what to do when you tell them to sit... great! Keep in mind that every time you teach your friend something new, the trust and bond between you grows stronger. The next command we will try is to follow you, one of the easier ones.

This can be done right after training your dog to sit, as they have been trained to sit down, you want them to stand up only when you say it's okay, which will help with future training techniques as well. Keep some treats in your pocket or hand, make sure your dog notices it and say the word "follow", or whichever word you prefer. Do not look back or stop, keep walking away for a bit, if your friend starts following you give them a treat.

This will be fairly easy, but be sure to adjust your movements. If your dog tries to run forward or in a different direction, turn and go the opposite way your dog is going and say follow, if they follow, provide some praise and a treat. Repetition is the key here, but this one should not take too long to master.

These are the basic things a dog and owner need in order for their relationship to be the best it can, and there will be less frustration when giving commands in later stages, as well as the bond that has formed during this training remaining and maybe even growing stronger as trust is gained.

Chapter 4:

True Discipline

Something you will start to notice when getting a dog is that the difference between having discipline yourself, and teaching discipline to your friend is not that different. When you think about it, you have to make the choice to get up and train your friend if you want them to listen, which takes great discipline to do over and over for a few weeks, and not everyone has the resolve for that.

For example, you start teaching your dog the sitting command. It's hot outside that day, more so than usual, your air conditioning isn't working or perhaps you don't have any, you don't want to go outside because the sun is burning bright, and so you decide to leave it for that day, because you can always do it tomorrow right? Well, that is true, sometimes due to circumstances, we just don't want to that day, and that's fine, but it's a slippery slope. Soon you realize you can just skip training altogether; who needs it anyway, am I right?

Well, you clearly do need it. Training your dog takes discipline, which you might not have–not everyone does. But teaching your dog might provide you with that discipline in return, that resolve to keep going as you see progress to that small glimmer of hope that in just a few days, you might be able to command your dog to get a beer out of the fridge for you while you sit and relax.

Let's take a look at how doing certain things might make training your dog easier, and in turn, make you a better, more productive person overall.

Discipline as the Owner

Keeping a good schedule is something many people suggest, even in everyday life, more so when training your dog. Remember, you are trying to teach your friend something that they may or may not grasp fairly quickly. In order for this to work out the best way possible, it is important to keep a schedule for training purposes.

Keep note of the times you are home, be it in the mornings or the evenings, or maybe you work from home, and then you have the whole day to plan out. When creating a training schedule, keep in mind the best time that suits you, as there is no need to impose on your own life just for the sake of training your dog. However, there is a chance that you will have to simply make time in order to train your dog. This schedule will also depend on the age of your new friend. If they are a bit older, you can start right away, but if it's a new puppy, it's best to wait a bit, starting with only the basics. Old or young, you will have to insist on the times you have set, otherwise, you might slip into forgetfulness or even just laziness, denying your friend their training.

Start your schedule by taking your friend outside for a bit, reinforcing companionship, and a toilet routine. While outside, you might consider playing a bit or continuing with some other training. Remember to give your dog their own time as well, so they can do as they please, otherwise they might become hopelessly dependent on you, which is not a good thing. Say you wanted to leave for the weekend and they cannot come with you. This might result in them being depressed.

Keeping to the training schedule is just as important as making it, and your dog will get used to the times of day you might leave home and return, reducing chances of them acting out. It will also help with basic training as you try to teach them something new at a specific time, and they will get used to needing to focus at these times.

In time, this will help you teach from example, and it might sound strange, but in the end, your dog might learn new mannerisms from the way you behave yourself. If you keep to the schedule you set up for you and your friend, your friend will be more likely to stick to it as well. Even when you act in a certain way towards people, your dog will detect this and may mimic you, as they can feel your intent, whether you like the person or not, and will act accordingly.

I remember I had this one friend, whom Chase did not quite like that much. Every time he visited, Chase would bark and go mad until I quieted him down and then moved him to the back yard. After a while, Chase became aware of what would happen when he acted that way towards my friend, and started gradually calming down by himself.

This also happens as your dog gets to know someone, as sometimes they are aggressive, but later on get used to their presence. This can be reinforced to ensure a more disciplined behavior, or be reinforced in the opposite way you desire, at which point the dog will automatically be more aggressive to strangers.

Keep in mind that dogs have a keen sense when it comes to human temperament, so when your dog does not like someone, there may be a reason for it. Maybe the person is exhibiting aggression or has ill intent that you do not realize. This is a common phenomenon where pets are usually able to pick up on when something just isn't right.

As mentioned before when we spoke about being the alpha, you will need to have strict discipline regarding this as well when training your dog. Especially when the dog is younger, if you exhibit submissive behavior towards your dog one day and dominant behavior the next, it might be a bit confusing to your dog, and result in them not quite understanding their place in your pack. Be firm in everything you say when dealing with your dog, and be sure about what you want your dog to do, so they will eventually pick up on what the score is.

So why does discipline even matter? This is a question that has both an obvious answer, and an obscure one. The obvious being that if your dog is disciplined, you will have an easier time controlling your friend and teaching them new commands.

The more obscure truth about discipline is that it gives a purpose to those who feel they have none. Maybe you are currently lost, not exactly sure where you are heading and what to do about it, and now you have a dog. Discipline will give you purpose; the purpose to train your dog, and just as you found a purpose, your dog will learn their purpose as well, following you and protecting you, maybe even being a friend to you.

I remember one day I was very angry when coming home, and I did not greet Chase when walking by him, I practically ignored him. This was not on purpose, it's just that I had other things on my mind, and I was distracted by my anger, which later developed into sadness. Chase picked up on this, and so he came to me in a docile manner, submissively laying next to me, trying to provide comfort and companionship. A dog with no discipline or purpose will not necessarily care enough to provide comfort. In fact, they might find this to be a good opportunity to challenge your authority. This leads us to the next part of this chapter.

Is Your Dog Disciplined?

The easiest way to tell if your dog is disciplined by now is whether or not they follow your commands the way they were trained. If you spent months training your friend, but they still do not perform these tasks as training, even when you know for a fact they know what you are asking of them, they might lack respect towards you. This sounds like a very strange concept for a dog to understand, but it is indeed true; they may decide to follow your commands, or disobey them.

The first thing to consider here is your dog's current state. If your dog has been a good boy or girl for the past few weeks, but now all of a sudden uses your favorite carpet as their toilet rug, the problem might not be discipline. If you trained your dog properly, and now out of the blue, they do not follow basic commands, there might be a bigger issue.

If this behavior occurs out of the blue, it might be a medical issue, and thus it would be best to take your friend to see a vet; a check-up never hurt anyone. On the other hand, your friend might be suffering from an emotional or psychological issue. Is there anything with which they can keep themselves busy? Have you been paying enough attention to them? More details regarding picking up on these things will be discussed in a later chapter, however, it is important to note when your dog's behavior changes for no reason.

If you have concluded there is no reasonable explanation of why your dog is behaving poorly, the cause might be you neglecting to enforce discipline in your dog's life. This was apparent with Chase in more than one way. I stayed with my father for a while, and on school holidays I would go stay with my mother. Every time I arrived there, I would notice that Chase had changed. It would take a bit of practice to have him properly follow commands again. The reason behind this was obvious, that no one reinforced these commands or rules when I was not there, and so he would adopt a whole new behavioral pattern.

So now your dog is not disciplined, and the reason is not medical or psychological, and you understand that you have been neglecting the schedule you set up for yourself. This is normal; we can't always perform at one hundred percent! Now, you need to make sure you do not lose your grip on your dog's discipline, and you have to punish your dog when they do something they may not, but how do you punish them? And when?

Every dog may be spanked in their life at some point; you might be annoyed that day and just can't handle the fact that your friend chewed on something they should not have, and you lose it, resulting in you hitting or spanking them. It is important to note that this will most likely not help the actual problem, so try to refrain from doing so, as your dog will start to associate you with pain and fear.

However, when you do catch your dog in the act of doing something they are not supposed to, it's fine to act aggressively and with intent, telling them firmly "no", tapping them lightly on the bottom. If they are chewing on something, take it away, and after a few minutes when the situation has calmed down, provide them with something that they are actually allowed to chew on. Provide some positive reinforcement when they start chewing on that. Keep in mind that you have to be firm when doing this, and you cannot be inconsistent. In the end, providing discipline and structure to your dog will make your life much easier in the future, and you will definitely reap the benefits when it comes to training your dog how to behave in public when you go for walks.

Your dog will start listening to you more attentively, responding much quicker to your commands. My father's pitbull, let's call him Buck, never really listened to me that much. When Buck would come to sit with me or play with me, he did so in a respectable and disciplined manner. However, when giving him commands, he didn't quite respond the way I wanted him to. It was only later on when I started paying more attention to the way I give him commands, and the way I handled his requests for attention, that he responded to my commands in a more controlled manner.

After a while, he started getting more protective over me as well; it was not just my father and stepmother that he tried to protect, I was now a part of his life more so than I was a few weeks prior. Simple details like this can make a big difference between you and your friend, as teaching and upholding discipline and structure is just as important as establishing an alpha in your pack.

If Not Discipline, What Else?

Discipline is not the only thing controlling your relationship with your dog.n fact, that would most likely lead to a very strict and cold relationship. Trust and love will play a major role as well.

First, the notion that dogs love unconditionally is quite inaccurate, and some people expect their dogs to love them from day one. Unfortunately, that's not how it works; love is earned, so if you feel your dog doesn't love you in the first few days, don't worry, it takes time! That is where training also comes in, helping solidify that bond between the two of you. Trust means you can leave your dog to their own devices for a while so they can relax with no training or bothersome commands, as well as protecting them when they need protection.

Chase used to be the top dog at my mother's house for quite a while, as it was only him and a small little dog my mother owned, a Miniature Pinscher I believe. He could do as he pleased, with no other dog getting in his way or stepping on his territory. Unfortunately for him, peace in his town would soon be disrupted.

My mother's little dog passed away at some point, and she became a little depressed as a result, until my stepfather decided to bring new dogs into our family, two English Bulldogs. Now, I did not quite like these two slobbering dogs lumbering around everywhere, and neither did Chase. In fact, they often bullied him as he was quite small in stature compared to them, and it was not the only thing to disturb his great kingdom; those two hounds had puppies.

Soon enough, little Chase was overwhelmed by all these new dogs, some of them growing bigger by the day. He would often come and seek protection from them, simply because they were annoying. They would walk around making a mess everywhere, they had no discipline, and I was not going to train them. Luckily for Chase, he could jump up to certain surfaces where they could not reach due to their… lethargy.

It is very important to provide protection for your dog should they come seeking it. This builds their trust in you, making it much more likely for them to comply when training. Comfort your dog while providing protection, reassuring them everything will be fine. Even when there is no visible danger or annoyance, no one knows your dog better than you, so if you know certain actions scare or annoy your friend, put a stop to them, should they come from another dog or human.

As mentioned above, no one knows your dog as well as you do, so why not learn what they like and don't like? When petting or scratching your dog, find that extra delightful spot they love so much. When playing, take note of what they like to do. Do they like to play fetch? Do they like chewing on something or maybe a little roughhousing? Make a point of focusing on these activities when it is playtime, especially after a training session, as it will positively reinforce everything that took place before playtime started. Keeping things strict when training is important, but remember to have fun! You are friends, aren't you?

Chase had this particular pastime to roll on the grass, and I observed this and decided to try it out on him. When playing, I would throw him over making him roll around on the bed, aggressively playing around with him. He enjoyed these sessions, as did I, with the end result being a much stronger bond.

Listening to what your dog has to say is a great way of understanding what they like, and how their personality functions. When you are going outside, and for some reason, your dog is refusing to join, try and understand why before thinking they are being disobedient. Maybe it's a bit cold or hot outside, maybe there is something in the yard that scares them, or they might not be feeling well. Paying attention is as much your responsibility as it is theirs. If you adopted a dog from a shelter, this is very important, as they might have had traumatic experiences, leading to them not wanting to perform a certain activity. So, for you to build a trusting relationship with them, you will have to listen to what they have to say. This ties in nicely with actually being there for your dog, being present in their world, and not just from a domineering perspective. When it's training time, commit to it, and when it's playtime, give it your all, and tire out your dog. Later, when you go relax, your friend will come and relax with you, and they won't care if they don't get attention because you gave them enough and now they just want to take a nap or relax by your side.

If you like exploring and going new to new places, try taking your dog with you. It's just as exciting for them, if not more, to see new places, smell new smells, and hear new sounds. This is also a good method to avoid your dog getting depression from being cooped up in the same place all the time.

True discipline does not come from commanding your dog and having them perform tricks for you. It comes from understanding each other, having the discipline to know when training is required and when playtime is needed. When you ask your dog to perform a certain feat, they do it because they trust and love you enough. You have displayed dominance over your friend, and they want to be sure you are worthy of being the alpha, which requires you to show not only true discipline, but true compassion as well.

Chapter 5:

Advanced Training

You know your dog better now, and after weeks of training and playing, you know what your dog likes and how they react to positive and negative reinforcement. Take some time to have your friend adjust to all of the training, and make sure they do not require treats anymore when complying with basic commands.

I would recommend at least 6 months after basic training is complete. This gives enough time for your pet to adjust, so now they don't react to commands simply because they will get a treat (although you can give them from time to time), but because they know that it is the way things are done, and that they get praised after.

In this chapter, we will cover quite a few things, ranging from public obedience to gestures, and even clicker training. The first being a quick look clicker training technique, and the other two exercises being "fetch" and "stay". These two are more basic commands, yet still complex concepts for your friend to understand. You can start a bit earlier with these two commands. Think of them as the bridge between the basic and advanced; these commands will determine whether or not you and your dog are ready for the more advanced stuff.

Clicker Training

I want to introduce you to this method of training before proceeding with further training, as it may help you a lot with future training endeavors.

Clicker training is quite interesting; it's a method of training very similar to basic positive reinforcement training. A clicker is simply a small device you manually use to produce a "click" sound, which goes a bit further into the science of positive reinforcement. Clicker training does not focus on what your dog is doing wrong at all; instead, it puts the spotlight on what your friend is doing right. So, in the end, you are pointing out what your dog should do, by clicking at exactly when your dog performed a task correctly.

This method works very well, especially when you have a more energetic friend who has a bit of trouble focusing. The click isn't anything special, it's similar to you praising your dog; the only difference is that the click is very prominent and can be easily heard by doggy ears (Stephanie Gibeault, MSc, 2019). What makes it such an effective method, is associating the click sound with a reward, and, in turn, associating specific mannerisms and tasks with the click. The reward that is received in the end is, as always, a treat or snack!

Do you remember what I said about Chase? He would jump onto any surface when I snap my finger. A snap, whistle, or clap can be substituted for the clicker. So if you wanted to start with this training, you will need some treats of course, and then either a clicker device or any form of easily detectable and identifiable sound creation method.

So let's teach your friend the new sound, and what exactly it means. This is quite easy; you simply have to create the sound, and provide your dog with a treat right after the sound. It would be best to downsize the treat portion for this type of training, as repetition is key here. You will have to click about 10 to 20 times a day, spreading them out evenly over the course of the day. Remember to provide a reward right after the sound was heard, and soon, after a few days, your friend will know that when they hear that sound, a reward will follow.

Using any form of gesture or sound that you prefer will work as well, but keep in mind that the gesture must be easily recognizable, and done the same way every time. While teaching this to your friend, you have to make sure they are focused every time you make the sound or gesture.

After you have now taught your friend the new sound or gesture, you can quickly start incorporating it into your other training. As an example, when training your friend how to sit, using the clicker every time they actually sit down will help them focus on what task they just performed, as they will want to do it again so that reward may follow. It is very important to produce the sound or gesture at the correct time, and provide the reward before your friend stands up. Clicker training is not a necessity when it comes to training your dog; it's simply a tool that makes it a bit easier.

This type of training can be used not just for teaching commands or basic training, but for changing your friend's behavior overall. Reinforcing good behavior will result in your dog behaving better in the future. For example, if your friend jumps up at guests, wait until they calm down and everyone is relaxed. Wait for your dog to sit down or lay down on the floor, and at this point, produce the sound or gesture and provide a reward. After a while, your dog will much rather stay relaxed when you have guests and will be less likely to jump up at them. If you don't like your dog begging around the table, ignore them, do not say anything or do anything. Simply wait for them to go and lay down. After a few minutes, you can produce the sound and provide the reward.

Most of your friend's behavioral patterns can be changed through this method. Eventually, when you finish training your friend something specific, or your dog is behaving themselves better after introducing a bit of positive reinforcement, you can stop with the sound or gesture. They will automatically respond better, complete the commands, and behave more disciplined. Should there be something new you want to teach, or their behavior slips, you can always start reintroducing the clicker method.

Play Time

Fetch is a game that comes a bit more naturally to some breeds than others. This makes sense, considering some dogs were bred for fetching, while others were bred for something completely different, so keep the breed of your dog in mind when training; especially the more advanced techniques, as that can affect the outcome and time it might take. Let's start teaching your friend about the favorite pastime of humans and dogs.

There are a few things needed to make training for fetch as smooth and fun as possible. The first thing to do is to find a toy to start with. If you have a few that you use in rotation, make sure you choose one specific toy and take it out of the rotation for now. It's best to stay with that one specific toy in the beginning, however, as training progresses, you can start choosing a toy from each rotation that can be used to play fetch with that day. Keep in mind that when training is finished, those toys can also be taken away from your dog should they act out while playing fetch later on.

The only other thing needed is treats. You can also use a clicker during this training, and it might make it easier if you have a breed who is not too interested in fetch. Teaching this game to your friend is a two-stage process, and again, this might be easier for some breeds to pick up on and more difficult for others. Keep in mind your dog's personality as well– maybe your friend is very lazy!

Teaching fetch starts off with the first stage, teaching your friend how to hold something. By now you may have a spot picked out where you and your friend are most comfortable when teaching new tricks or to simply play around, but don't worry if you don't, it's not necessary, however, it does help if both of you are in a comfortable spot. Just like when training to sit, you will want to be right in front of your friend, preferably with no other distractions around. You can sit down if you like, with your chosen toy in hand, and if it's a new one your dog hasn't seen yet, it might be easier.

Hold out the new toy, and when your friend comes forward to investigate this new smell, praise your friend or use your clicker. If they are not too interested, bring it closer to their nose, and when they start sniffing, you can praise/click or use treats as a form of praise. Now, since interest has been established in this new item, see if you can get your friend to try and lick or bite it; should he or she comply, you may praise/click. If your friend is being a bit stubborn, you can try and take a break, or take the time to check in on what mood your friend is in... maybe he/she is tired. Maybe your dog is not responding well, and that's OK You can try and rub the treat over the toy and hold them out together, and your friend will most likely start responding better.

After your dog has realized they get rewarded for biting this item, try to slowly increase the duration between the time your friend bites it, and the time you praise/click. Increasing the duration slowly is quite important and will definitely help later on, so start with a second, and then a second and a half, and so on. After doing this a couple of times, you can start using a word like "hold" or "carry", which will eventually replace the praise/click.

As you continue praising/clicking and using your chosen word or gesture, you can add to the duration of time they hold the item for you, but only by half seconds. Make sure you hold the item in your hand so they don't try and run off with it. After your friend gets used to holding it for a few seconds, you can start taking your hand off as well, quickly going back to holding it, so they won't try and run off or maybe drop it. You can then start increasing the duration between you letting go and grabbing it again.

This is where you start having your friend properly let go as well. Unfortunately, most people make the mistake of not training their dogs to actually let go of the item when trying to teach them to fetch. When you take the item away from your friend, praise/click as they let go. This will make sure they understand that letting go means reward, you can start adding in the words "let go" after a few tries. You have to do this very slowly as well, adding the right increments of time between holding and taking or letting go.

A pattern that works quite well is when you do a few quick holds, and one for a longer period of time, after which you do a few quick ones again, gradually replacing the quick ones for longer ones. Your friend is now a master of holding things and letting them go.

We can move onto the next stage of teaching your friend the art of 'fetch'.

Start off holding the item out to your dog and ask them to hold it for you, and depending on how the training went, your friend will most likely take it out of your hand and hold it for you. If this is not the case, don't worry. You can simply go back to the first stage and practice some more. If your dog did indeed take the item, praise/click and add in a treat for good measure. Take the item back, and place it on the ground, tell your friend to hold and praise/click if they do so, and if not, you can try telling your friend to hold while you start placing it on the ground. Taking your time when trying to get your friend to hold it earlier will really pay off around this time, as they will hold the item even if not in your hand, or at least try to do so with more haste. If at this point, your dog picks up the item readily and consistently, you can start placing the item a bit further away from you, but not too far at first. Remember to praise your friend every time they pick it up, and every time they give it back when you ask them to.

You can take a break after having your friend pick it up a few times, as to make sure they do not lose focus. After a while, you can start increasing the distance and start to throw it, instead of placing it on the ground, but do not throw it far—only a few feet away. You can start repeating this cycle of throwing it, telling your friend to hold, and then asking them to give it back. While your friend gets used to the idea of what this game entails, you can start using the word fetch if you want, swapping it out for hold. It's a good strategy to start swapping the item for another, should you wish to have more than one toy allowed to be used for fetch.

Now your friend knows how to hold, give, and in the end, play fetch. This is where discipline can become interesting, and you can start getting your friend used to "fetch" by playing every day, still providing treats occasionally and finally moving on to no treats. You can start incorporating other commands into this as well, testing the discipline of your friend. Perhaps have them sit before running off and getting the item you threw.

It is quite simple, but it teaches your dog context, and they will be easier to control in public areas when they have a more complex idea of when commands can apply. However, after all the training and commands, it will be second nature for both of you. This is where playtime is fun, as the two of you don't spend time learning, but rather, you bond through playing together and enjoying it.

Stay!

Stay is often regarded as one of the more difficult commands for a dog to learn, as they always want to be with you! However, it does prove useful in public areas and has simple applications at home.

The key to teaching your friend to stay is to make sure there is a beginning to the stay period, and an ending. This may sound obvious, but it is not to your friend, so make sure you have a word for having them stay, and a word for letting your friend know they can stop sitting in the same place. Teaching the stay command is fairly simple in the sense that they will recognize the word, and then sit or lay down. The hard part is making sure they won't follow as soon as you walk away.

In order for you to teach your friend to stay, you can adopt the same tactic as when teaching your friend to fetch, increasing the time and distance slowly. Have your friend memorize the stay command = through praise/clicking every time they sit down when given the command. After this, you can start backing away slowly, starting with only a few feet. After backing away, you can sound the release word. You can use some gestures to excite your friend so they may run towards you, so remember to provide praise every time your friend stays, and when they come to you after giving the command. You can increase the distance slowly, and even start turning around, but you will have to be patient when going through this, otherwise it will not work.

Soon you will reach the point where you can go around the corner and they will still stay, however, it does take time, so just be sure to take it slow when starting with the first few feet.

What About the Rest?

After going over basic dog training, discipline, training techniques, and clicking, there is not much for you to learn as the owner; the only thing left is to teach your friend new commands, should you wish to do so. Let's go over some of the more advanced commands and behavior changes that may require you to utilize the skills you both have learned..

Public discipline - Depending on your personal preference, you might want to take your friend out for a walk to the park, maybe a jog, or just a fun time on the beach. These are all great ideas, and are encouraged by most people, however, you need to be sure you can control your dog, should any situation demand it. This can range from meeting a stranger, meeting another dog, going somewhere by car, or even being threatened by a stranger.

First of all, it's a good idea to get your friend used to other dogs. This can be done by either having more than one dog, or by arranging puppy play dates with other friends and their pets. This may also prevent depression in your friend's future as well, as going out to play with other dogs if you do not own more than one can help a lot. What may help as well is training with a leash; make sure your friend understands that when you tug on the leash, they should calm down.

Call – Something basic but also not always positively reinforced, is when your dog actually comes to you when you call them, Make sure to always praise/click when they come running when you call their name. This can be used in unison with specific sounds or gestures.

No food from strangers – Another interesting addition to your dog's training is to make sure they do not take food from strangers. This can be applied in public, as well as when you are not home, and someone tries to poison your dog. This can be taught in unison with the stay command after your friend has mastered stay, and you can have a friend try and entice them with a treat. Do this by having someone hold a treat out for a few seconds after you gave the stay command. Then, when they put the treat away, you may then praise/click. Should your dog try and move or go towards them, keep giving the stay command, and if they do move, have your friend put the treat away immediately. After a few tries, your dog will not try and eat something provided by strangers, at least to a certain degree.

Heel – Similar to the "follow" command, the only difference being that heel can be taught while using a leash, making it perfect for public application. You can do this by having a few treats with you while walking around the house or yard, then call your friend to your side and keep walking while holding the treat beside you. Make sure to say the word "heel", or whichever word you prefer, as they follow you on your side. You can do this with a gesture as well, and while doing it with a leash, you can keep them in place next to you. This will help if you are walking in public and your dog seems a bit too excited. Saying the command will have them walk right back at your side.

Most commands and behavior can be reinforced through positive feedback, so when you and your friend have mastered the basics, and at least one advanced command, it will become easier to communicate, as you understand each other more easily than before, and your bond has grown stronger.

Think of these advanced techniques as a key, with which you can unlock your own training methods according to your dog's personality.

Chapter 6:

A Brief Look at Professional Training

Many people have heard about service dogs. Some people know what that means, and others are not entirely sure. No matter the reason, in the end, these dogs have received the best training possible so as to achieve the best possible result when taking care of their human friends.

The main objective for a service dog is usually to help their owner, who will most likely suffer from a certain disease, disorder, illness, or disability. Service dogs may only be assigned to people who meet the legal requirements set by their region or country. From a more technical view, service dogs are there to help in the area in which their owner is lacking, be it with sight, hearing, mobility, or notifying their owner of either blood-related issues or allergens.

Now we have only discussed civilian service dogs, however, we also have service dogs in the military and police, providing more than just assistance, but as in the wars discussed, also giving their lives in order to protect us. In this chapter, we will be taking a brief look at what types of service dogs there are exactly and what each of their responsibilities might be, including the training required to reach the highest point in their career.

Looking back, the first service dogs on record were around during the time of the Roman Empire in Pompeii. Found there was a Frieze depicting a blind man being guided by a dog. For reference, a Frieze is a sort of decorative architectural band that you might find at the top of a door or establishment, usually against the wall right underneath the ceiling. Archeologists have also uncovered a scroll in China which is believed to have been painted around the 13th century. In this scroll, a dog is depicted as guiding an old man through a very busy and obscure street.

There are a few other accounts of dogs in service in the past. One being a Color Stipple-engraving done by Italian artist Thomas Gaugain, depicting a young blind girl being guided through the countryside by her furry friend in the 17th century. In 1780, a hospital for the blind called Les Quinze-Vingts started training dogs in order to facilitate a more comfortable environment for the patients.

Over the last 100 years, many things were learned when it came to service dog training, some of them discovered through training a whole different species. The effectiveness of positive reinforcement was discovered through the behavioral training of dolphins, and soon the information was widespread amongst dog trainers, and became the best-known method.

What Levels Are There?

Starting off, we obviously get the basic civilian service dog level. Now, I am not taking anything away from our furry friends when I say basic level, as the training required to reach this level alone is astonishing.

Civilian service dogs, better known as assistant dogs, can be split into quite a few categories. But rather than do that, let's take a look at the most required types of assistant dogs. The list is ever-changing as we discover new conditions that may need assistance, and how we train our friends to better deal with these situations.

Let's start with the basic guide dog. Guide dogs are very simply what the name implies; they guide their visually-impaired owners through their homes, public spaces, and any other obstacles that might appear.

The guide dog is the backbone, so to speak, of most service dog positions, and is the oldest-known position. The most commonly seen breed in this position is usually the Labrador Retriever and Golden Retriever, with a mix of the two also being a popular option. A rather new addition to the roster for guide dogs is the Poodle. There are exceptions to some breeds, but these three are usually the ones best suited for the job.

Next up is the hearing assistance dog. Many people, unfortunately, suffer from hearing impairments and do not always end up being compatible with a technological solution. Even when a compatible solution is found, an assistance dog may still be recommended, should the hearing aids fail, or for other uses and assistance. The service rendered by these assistants will range from alerting their owner to specific sounds such as alarms or doorbells.

The most popular breeds in this regard are Labrador Retrievers and Golden Retrievers as well. However, there are many cases in which the use of Cocker Spaniels and Miniature Poodles have proven successful. According to some reports, there have been cases where Terrier mixes and Chihuahuas were compatible with the training and their owners due to personality traits and specific temperament.

Third, we have mobility assistance dogs, who will usually assist with a wide range of mobility-related problems caused by either accidents or conditions from birth. These can range from spinal cord injuries to arthritis, and in these cases, the dogs will assist with fetching certain items, or even interacting with certain objects, such as buttons and switches. One of the usual requirements of mobility assistance dogs is that they must be a large enough size in order to assist with physical support as well.

Next, we have one of the more interesting service dog positions. We all know how keen a dog's senses can be, and these friends of ours can help alert diabetic humans of chemical changes in their blood sugar. There are certain chemical events in your blood that remain undetected by us, but these changes leave a faint scent, and our furry helpers can detect and alert us when this happens. So, in their case, they will alert their owner, or even someone else in the house, so that a test can be done.

Seizure alert and seizure response dogs are in another category of very interesting service dogs. The two are not to be confused as their names suggest, as they have two very different forms of assistance to be delivered. Though the evidence supporting seizure alert dogs is quite scarce, nonetheless, many families, trainers, and owners have come to realize and stand by the fact that having a friend alert them right before a seizure might occur, is quite helpful. The ability to detect these seizures seems to be a natural ability, however, as I have mentioned, the evidence surrounding these claims is not very substantial.

The seizure response dogs do exactly as the name suggests. These dogs are trained to act immediately, should the first signs of a seizure appear. They will alert anyone nearby who may be able to help, and bring medication or a cellphone to their owner once the seizure has subsided, should there be no one around. Depending on the size of the dog, they might also be trained to move their owner out of unsafe areas and protect them should it be necessary.

Another category in which service dogs help humans every day is through emotional and psychiatric support. Dog owners know just how emotionally uplifting it can be when you come home from a long day of work, finding your furry friend at home happy to see you. Service dogs take this a step further by providing emotional support for their owners that went through traumatic experiences. Humans suffer from a great deal of mental and emotional stress. PTSD is one of the main conditions treated through the use of a service dog. Should their human companions feel stressed, overwhelmed, or anxious, the dogs will try and isolate them from what is causing the episode.

On the other side of psychiatric service dogs are the ones who help children with severe autism. These dogs will try to create predictable scenarios in social situations so that the child may socially navigate easier. The dogs provide them with emotional support should they feel alone, and also try to reduce isolation from social events. These dogs are also trained trackers. Should the child run away, their assigned dog will be able to find them and make sure to alert someone should something happen to the child. All assistance dogs retire when they reach a certain age, they are usually taken back to where they were trained in order to find them a proper home with a loving family, where they can relax for the rest of their lifespan.

Of course, as we discovered in chapter one, we get more than just civilian service dogs. There are a few branches in public safety and military which have a need for service dogs in many different fields.

Starting with general police dogs, the preferred breed will usually be German Shepherds, however, you can also expect to see Bloodhounds, Dutch Shepherds, Belgian Malinois, and Labrador Retrievers as part of police and military forces. With the basic task of suspect apprehension, the dogs and their handlers are usually referred to as K9-units (get it?), with basic training covering how to catch, bite, and hold down fleeing suspects. These dogs are usually the first to put their lives on the line, as they run out towards danger to ensure capture and subjugation. These furry enforcers are trained to know who is a threat and who is not, and they are usually very calm under pressure and respond only to their handlers' commands.

If you try and hide a treat from your dog, the likelihood that they will sniff it out is quite considerable. Playing into this keen sense of theirs, humans have trained many dogs for detecting criminal substances such as drugs or explosives. They are not always bound to specific areas, as they can be deployed at airports, borders, big events, or even at a local parking area when searching civilian vehicles. Taking this a step further, military units have dogs like Bak with them as well, for detecting landmines and explosives, as we learned in chapter one.

A less action-packed, but by no means less important, job these dogs have is for search and rescue. Some people end up getting lost when hiking, leaving it up to these professionally trained dogs to find them. They are trained to find these people, whether alive or deceased, even when buried underground or snow. The amount of precision these dogs have when searching for someone can make search and rescue much easier, as they can cover larger areas more quickly and more accurately.

We covered civilian and police dogs, but we cannot discuss service dogs without mentioning military-trained service dogs, many of which have been key players in taking down infamous terrorists. Most people are familiar with the fact that military-trained canines exist in the army, navy, and airforce, however, there exists a unit of dogs even higher up the chain, the special multi-purpose canine. If you think military, you might think of the basic infantryman and then the special forces, who are the best of the best, and that is where these furry beasts come into play.

When talking about the American military, these dogs will be found in Navy SEAL units, Army Rangers, the US Marines, and Delta Force units. These special forces canines are not limited to the American military however, and can be found in many other countries all over the world.

These multi-purpose canines (MPCs) are trained just as the name suggests, covering a wide range of duties and skills, such as helicopter rappelling, parachute jumps, and a wide variety of water-related operations. As mentioned, these MPCs have played their roles in anti-terrorist operations, the most recognized dog being "Cairo", who assisted in the raid that took down Osama bin Laden.

Not just any dog can enter into these ranks, but unfortunately, due to the level of secrecy surrounding the operations in which they participate, the training methods used are classified. What we do know is that the dogs are trained very strictly with their handlers, as no barking is allowed and they are able to stay calm during firefights. The selection process is very strict, and a team of veterinarians, handlers, and trainers will scout around for dogs, checking for any medical conditions that might hinder their service in the foreseeable future. Dogs with any bone defects, eye defects, hearing problems, and skin conditions are automatically ruled out. This is only the physical examination of the selection process, as they will be further checked on their temperament, natural ability, and trainability.

These heroes to their respective countries retire after a certain amount of combat missions or when they are injured severely. Some dogs even return to service after they are treated. When retiring, they are examined to make sure there are no signs of PTSD, and that they pose no threat to the public or to their future caretakers, after which they are placed in homes where they are taken care of by a loving family until old age.

Where to Get A Service Dog

We now know what services these dogs can provide for us, but what if you are in need of a service dog? Or maybe you want to train your own service dog? What are the requirements to become a service dog in the first place?

There are many breeding programs out there specializing in providing the best possible service dog breeds. These dogs are trained to deal with daily distractions and are very reliable, making it much easier for trainers to work with them, resulting in a better experience for the person in need of such a dog.

There are many training centers around the world that provide the public with access to pre-trained dogs, and courses for training dogs that are brought in. The cost related to having your dog trained or getting a pre-trained service dog can vary extensively, depending on the breed, country, and whether it is a non-profit or profit training center. As a rough estimate, service dogs can cost up to fifty thousand US dollars, and this is only the estimate for training, not accounting for yearly costs of food, check-ups, and additional training. So when looking for a service dog, make sure to do your research about the company you might want to approach.

Getting a service dog is fairly easy, as it just depends on the level of training you require from them, your disability or emotional condition, and budget. Depending on the laws of your specific country or region, you might require an official medical letter stating the reason for your application, or you may even train your own service dog.

The Law

Service dogs are found all over the world, and should you encounter one, do not try to get their attention or pet them. Some dogs might wear vests that explain this, however, not everyone takes the warning seriously. When you do see a dog in a vest, it is also not necessarily a service dog. The law surrounding vests vary between regions, however, generally, service dogs and emotional support dogs are not accounted for under the same laws. For example, there is a distinct difference between a dog helping their owner deal with emotional stress by simply being present, and dogs who are trained to sense anxiety and react accordingly.

Both of these dogs might be wearing vests, however, only the one trained is approved for public access. This is the same for dogs who are in service of someone with a disability and are trained to either perform or help with specific tasks. There are even appointed courtroom dogs in order to support children or emotionally traumatized adults, delivering statements or during trial proceedings. These dogs however are not recognized as official service dogs and thus, the laws surrounding them are different.

Now, unfortunately, there are people who try and take advantage of this system, trying to state that the dog they have with them is indeed a service dog when they are not. Special accommodations are offered to people with actual disabilities and dogs who help them with everyday life, and some people want to exploit that for their own gain, causing confusion. It may also result in damages if their untrained or improperly trained dogs are allowed into public spaces where they otherwise may not have access to.

Something I must ask you as a dog owner, and a citizen who respects authority, is to not try to interact with service dogs in public unless given permission, and to not try and pass your dog as a service dog if they are not, in order to get access to otherwise cordoned off areas. This greatly hurts the system put in place, and disrespects the intense training these dogs go through, and the effort the trainers themselves go through, to keep this system running smoothly.

Chapter 7:

Taking Care of Your Friend

Taking care of your furry friend throughout your lives together may seem like something obvious to do, however, not everyone realizes the ramifications of getting a new dog. My stepbrother, for example, brought Chase to us with no real plan, and in the end, he neglected to take care of him the way he should have. He never fed him–my mother would always do that–and he gave him very little attention, leaving it to me and my other family members.

There are many things that may happen that you will have to be ready to deal with, whether it be an injury, sickness, or even old age. Plan ahead so that you do not get stuck in a situation where you can no longer take care of your friend the way they deserve.

Something to consider as well is that technology is a great thing, and can help you find your friend should they get lost, even after you did what you could. Sometimes they will find a way, no matter how hard you try, and that is not your fault. The only thing you can do is to get a little help from technology. It's recommended to have a collar and tag on your dog, which is legally enforced in some areas. Additionally, microchips and GPS tracking tags can help you even more.

Starting with the microchip, it's a small rice-grain-sized chip injected into the loose skin of your friend, similar to a vaccine, so as not to worry about invasive surgery. This chip carries a unique identification number which, if scanned, can tell the vet or shelter to whom the dog belongs. The GPS tag is a bit more extreme; however, if you know your friend likes exploring, this might be a good option. Some tags even offer the option to monitor and record the daily movement of your dog. It's also a great option should you take your friend out hiking or exploring with you, just in case.

In the end, it will all be up to you to make sure you are prepared as much as you can be.

Your Dog, Your Responsibility

A few years ago, before Chase became a part of the family, we had two other dogs. One being the Miniature Pinscher my mother adores, and the other a big and quite old English Bulldog. The bulldog came from my stepfather's side, and soon after joining the new family dynamic, he started having some trouble doing his business outside.

We started to hypothesize as to why this may be... was it the stress? Was it due to all the new people? About a week passed since this issue started, and finally reached a point where it started getting worse. We decided to take him to a vet in order to find out what might be wrong, and we were quite surprised. After the initial checkup and some further tests, the vet informed us that he had a bowel obstruction, and that if we had brought him in any later, he might not have made it.

We were having trouble piecing together how this might have happened, nonetheless, we made sure he got all better through proper treatment and medication afterward. When we got home after it all, we started to form the bigger picture as we conversed around the topic. My stepfather told us that the dog used to have an obsession with chewing random items he found laying around, and due to the lack of proper discipline and training, this behavior persisted. I started to recall seeing small pieces of tree bark laying around the yard, and these pieces were usually left in the flower beds; something so obvious that went completely unnoticed.

In the end, he was chewing on the bark he found out of stress, due to the big move and massive change in lifestyle. We were all so busy that we never noticed he might be stressed or devoid of attention, resulting in him chewing and swallowing all the bark he could find. Luckily, we did take notice of his sudden change in routine, so we managed to get him some help just in time. He lived for a few more years, eventually passing away due to old age.

This was a major lesson for us, as we started to realize the emotional strain big events can have on the dogs around us. As humans, we have only recently started to take notice of the emotional and psychological range dogs have, and the ways they express them. This plays a large part in taking care of your friend. Making sure they are healthy is no longer just up to their state of physical being, but the psychological state as well.

I remember one day I had to take Chase to the vet, as my parents were out of town that weekend. Ever since he was a puppy, he had this obsession with scratching his ear. Now, this was never an issue, and we were reassured by a vet that it should subside, which it did. However, every now and then he would start scratching again, and during this particular weekend, it reached a point where he let out a small wincing sound as he scratched. This was my first time noticing it, and after what happened with the bulldog, I did not want to take a chance. Chase has a poor history of going to vets, however, I have never taken him myself. When putting him in the car I immediately noticed him shaking, and I started to calm him down and reassure him nothing bad was going to happen. By the end of the trip there and back, he behaved himself very well all around, even when we were in the waiting room.

The smaller dog my mom had came with her own health issues, and unfortunately, at an older age, she started developing a heart condition, as many miniature species might. We actually found her on our way to our new home, where she was badly hurt and left for dead next to the road. My mother decided to keep her, which ended up being a good choice, as she integrated well with the family. Due to her small size, however, there were a few times she disappeared on us, and we had no idea where she went. Eventually, we found her escape route, which was a small hole in the fence she would use to explore during the day, and then return at night. We closed up the hole for fear of her running away and not finding her way back, or worse.

There are three main reasons I shared these stories with you.

One being, you need to realize the responsibility you are taking upon yourself when getting a dog. You need to be vigilant and perceptive of your dog's physical and emotional well-being; otherwise, you might unknowingly impair your friend's health. In this chapter, we will discuss telltale signs of certain psychological conditions, as well as symptoms presented by specific illness or disease.

Secondly, your friend needs you to be there for them, especially at times when things are changing around you. When getting a dog, you have to be sure that you will be there to play with them, provide companionship, or at least have someone around when you are not there for extended periods of time.

Thirdly, as discussed in chapter 2, you must be prepared for anything when getting a dog. Be sure to check your house and surrounding area for anything that your dog might have access to, whether it's something they might eat or a hole they can scurry into.

The day might come when you cannot find your dog, at which point you might hear a crash, run outside, and find that someone accidentally ran over your friend. This is a very difficult topic to discuss, but what will happen now? Are you going to blame the driver for not noticing your very fast and small friend? Maybe the driver was on their phone, or maybe they did see your dog and tried to stop in time but couldn't. Whose fault was it in the first place?

Did you make sure there are no holes in the fence? Did you forget to close your front door? You have to be prepared to accept responsibility for when you make a mistake that results in the injury or death of your friend. However, even more so, you need to make sure there is no way of it happening in the first place. Maybe it was the driver's fault, but maybe, there is a hole in the fence you meant to get fixed, and just never committed the time to do so.

The same applies to the type of food you feed to your dog, the snacks you give them, and the training you provide them. You should know the limits your friend has when training, and there is no point in trying to force them. You may count on your friend for many things, but keep in mind that they rely on you for a safe, healthy, and friendly environment. Just because the world out there is crazy, doesn't mean we have to live with that crazy in our homes with our furry friends.

It is your responsibility, and no one else's.

Diet and Grooming

One of the ways to ensure you and your dog live happily ever after is by providing them with the proper diet! There are so many foods on the market these days, ranging from cheap to expensive, wet to dry, and then, of course, there is also human food.

It's important to realize that this is not a one-size-fits-all deal, as some dogs will respond to certain food brands differently than how your neighbor's dog might respond. My friend used to have two dogs (I cannot recall the breeds as they were mixed); but I do remember that the one was quite large and the other quite small. This brought forth an interesting problem for my friend, as he had to buy two different types of dog food. Nevermind the size difference and the amount that each dog consumed, but they both had their own preferred food! Now that I think about it, they were quite spoiled, which is not necessarily a bad thing, just make sure it is regulated.

Your friend's diet is not influenced by just what he or she prefers or not, but how their body reacts to the food as well. How do you know what food to get? Well, most brands work, as they are, after all, sold as food for dogs, but let's take a more in-depth look at how you can determine the best food for your friend. First, do not trust advertisements, as they might seem genuine. But keep in mind, they are only there to make sure you buy it. When buying dog food, rather, read the nutritional label on the packet or bag. Doing this will provide you with a much better idea of what food is better than the other, and which will ultimately be the better option for your friend. Alternatively, you can always do your own research or ask your local vet for their opinion on the current food you are providing to your dog.

Something to keep in mind is that you should not consider shelf-stable food as the main source of nutrients for your dog. These products do provide nutrients; however, they lack specific enzymes which can be considered as "live", due to the process of making it shelf-stable. This is not to say you cannot use them at all, as they are still good sources of nutrition for your dog, but try and mix a few other things in between.

Speaking of mixing other food items in, if you are wondering what you might be able to add to your friend's diet in order for them to be as healthy as possible, think of fruit and vegetables. These are great sources of fiber and vitamins, as well as for those "live" enzymes, as they are naturally grown. As I am sure you have heard, some fruits and veggies can be bad for your pet, so let's briefly go over the best nutritious and safe ones, as well as the bad ones that may end up being poisonous, as the worst-case scenario. I do also advise doing some more research on the subject in order to find the best fruits and veggies for your friend.

Apples, bananas, and oranges are some of the easiest fruits to come by, and luckily, they are all safe for ingestion and full of nutrients for your dog. Be sure to remove the core and seeds from the apple and the skin from the oranges. Due to the high content of sugar, the bananas are best left as a treat and not as a main food source. Mangos and peaches are fine as well, but remember to remove the seed/stone from the center as it contains a small amount of cyanide, and might become a choking hazard. Do not give grapes, cherries, and raisins to your friend, as these can be very poisonous and could be fatal, to the point where they could suffer from acute kidney failure soon after eating them.

Moving on to some veggies, the most readily available ones like broccoli, brussel sprouts, carrots, and green beans are safe for your dog's consumption, and will provide many benefits. Keep in mind the size of your friend to avoid any choking hazards along the way. Avocados are not recommended for your dog, as they cause diarrhea, due to a high volume of the toxin, persin. Tomatoes are another veggie/fruit that should be avoided. Even though it is safe for dogs to ingest a ripe tomato, there is a toxin known as solanine which is contained in the green parts, so rather avoid them just to be safe.

You can give some raw meat to your dog as well, however, as some chemicals are created when doing so, it can increase the chance of your friend getting cancer.

So your friend has a healthy and nutritious diet—what else can be done to make sure he or she stays healthy? Make sure your dog is well-groomed! This might sound silly, but think of it this way: if you are dirty, the chances of picking up an infection are much higher. So, bathe your friend at least once or twice a month. Contrary to what most believe, it is actually good to bathe your friend at least once or twice a week! However, not everyone has the time or necessarily the patience for that, so once or twice a month will do, unless your friend is noticeably more dirty some days.

Clipping their nails is also something that many people neglect or forget about. If you do not see yourself doing that, or are unable to, take them to a groomer or vet to do so. When their nails start to touch the ground when standing, they need a clipping! The same can be said for teeth cleaning. Many owners forget to clean their dog's teeth every now and then. But it does not have to be a chore, as some chewable treats and toys help do this for you.

Possible Conditions and Afflictions

There are many causes and symptoms to many different medical problems your dog might face, and it is your responsibility to look out for these symptoms and make sure your dog is properly treated medically . Just the other day, my friend's dog started developing a strange skin problem, and we later found out that this was due to an allergic reaction from the new dog food my friend had bought!

Now, some conditions may relate to your dog's health and breed, so it is best to do some research regarding these things, especially when you notice behavioral changes in your friend. There are, however, a few common problems that can be identified quickly and treated swiftly. One of the most common health issues is ear infections, which can be identified when your dog paws at their ear a lot, as Chase did.

Fleas and ticks are another well-known and easily identifiable problem among canines. If you suspect your friend might have either of these, do a proper inspection of their skin and bedding to be sure. Luckily, it's easily treatable through a wide range of medications, drops, powders, and collars. One of the more serious parasites to worry about is heartworm. These parasites will grow inside your dog's heart and lungs, living off the ample blood supply available. It is a bit more difficult to identify, so if your dog has a strange cough, seems fatigued, and is not really interested in anything, get them to a vet for a checkup! Modern vaccines do prevent this from happening, so it is recommended to stay up-to-date with all shots!

A more obscure disease is kennel cough, which is, as the name suggests, common in dogs that have spent significant time at a vet or shelter. The basic symptom is coughing and hacking constantly, and there is no real way to prevent it, similar to the common cold for humans, so all you can do is make sure they get some rest and proper nutrition–it will blow over!

There are more severe health issues from which your friend might suffer, such as cancer, arthritis, cataracts (which can be present from birth), kidney problems, the list goes on. In any case, if you notice your friend is not well, or their behavior changed completely and has not gotten better in a few days, get them to the vet! It's better to do a check-up than to leave your friend to suffer with no help!

Emotional and Psychological Health

Just like you and me, our pets may suffer from a mental disability or emotional trauma. It might not be as common, but it does happen. The best way to avoid this from happening is by simply being a friend to your furry friend!

Common mental disorders may range from depression, to many forms of anxiety, canine compulsive disorder (CCD), or severe stress. These disorders listed are fairly easy to detect, so let's take a look at what signs you should look out for if you suspect your dog might have some trauma or psychological problems.

When talking about the many forms of anxiety, they can be listed as separation anxiety, which is when they feel they might be left alone. Social anxiety can cause dogs to be very nervous when around other dogs or humans, and is a result of being left alone for extended periods of time. Noise anxiety is fairly common in many breeds and can be seen as their behavior changes when loud noises such as thunderstorms or fireworks occur. Most forms of anxiety will be shown through trembling, hiding, compulsive licking, or destructive behavior.

Depression can sometimes be a bit more difficult to detect; however, it is very important to pay attention to our friends, as they cannot exactly tell us. This is usually avoided when they have another dog to play with, or if they spend a lot of time with their owners. Depression can be detected though, so should you see your friend lost his or her appetite, reduced activity and seem lethargic, or experienced drastic weight loss, try and do some cheering up! If it does not work and they refuse all manner of playtime and treats, get them to a vet for some professional advice, as there might be something else wrong.

In the end, your dog's emotional health will depend on you, so do not leave them alone for extended periods of time, and make sure you play with them if there are no other dogs. If you do not have time to play with your friend due to a work situation, have someone else take your dog for walks, or try and arrange a playdate.

Our furry friends provide us with such happiness in a world so crazy, it's sometimes impossible to see the happiness and support with which they provide us. We have to be there for them as well, to make sure they are not left alone and unhappy, in order to make sure they are healthy and eating well. It is our duty and responsibility as owners, and as friends.

Conclusion

This should be the part where I cover everything we have gone over, have you recall what you have learned, and what knowledge you've retained from your reading experience. I do not want to do that, as the conclusion to a book about training and caring for your dog is, in the end, not about you.

It is about our furry friends.

We have seen what dogs have done for us when we were at our lowest point as humans, and we have seen how we have embraced our furry friends' companionship. We know how important they are to our society as a whole, and why we need them to be there for us, just as they need us. We now know how to feed them, how to train them, and how to care for them.

Dogs are fascinatingly supportive, understanding, instinctively compassionate, and are fierce companions. This is a fact, and the only reason we still find dogs who act aggressively towards humans is because their owners either abandoned them, mistreated them, or improperly trained them. This is a very sad reality, however, it is a reality that can be shaped by our will to improve it. We can decide to treat our friends better, in the same way they treat us, with compassion and patience.

The day will come when Chase passes on and goes to doggy heaven, and it will be a sorrowful day; however, I will never regret the time I spent with him, trying to train him properly when others neglected to do so. I will never forget that time spent, as it created a bond that will never be broken, a bond that will remain after he passes away. This is the reality I wish upon all dog owners, to experience the companionship of a friend to whom you tried your best to give a meaningful and joyful life.

You do not have to train your dog to be the most disciplined multi-purpose canine out there, and you do not need to spend all your money on them, as they will love you either way. This is the blessing that was given to us in a world that mostly takes away. Dogs provided us with a way to better ourselves as humans, whether we are at home, in public, on the battlefield, or playing in the backyard.

There are so many things these days that change around us, as technology progresses at an alarming rate, bringing us closer to the feared singularity. Our environment is changing as we move forward with industrial projects. There is, however, one thing that will not change for as long as they exist, which is our furry friends' abilities to be there when we need them the most.

Taking care of your friend is your responsibility as their owner, it is your duty as their guardian, and it is your privilege as their friend—there is no excuse not to do so. I can promise you if you provide them with love, food, and shelter, training them will be easy, as they will want to be a better dog just for you.

References

A brief history of dogs in warfare. (2017, March 20). Military.Com. https://www.military.com/undertheradar/2017/03/brief-history-dogs-warfare

Dog training: How to train a dog & dog obedience training (2017). American Kennel Club. https://www.akc.org/expert-advice/training/

Handwerk, B. (2018, August 15). *How accurate is alpha's theory of dog domestication?* Smithsonian; Smithsonian.com. https://www.smithsonianmag.com/science-nature/how-wolves-really-became-dogs-180970014/

Opinion: We didn't domesticate dogs. they domesticated us. (2013, March 3). Nationalgeographic.Com. https://www.nationalgeographic.com/news/2013/3/130302-dog-domestic-evolution-science-wolf-wolves-human/

Phivo Christodoulou. (2017, August 9). *15 Tips to improve your dog's diet today.* Dogs Naturally. https://www.dogsnaturallymagazine.com/15-tips-improve-dogs-diet-today/

J. K. (2019). *Service dogs 101: Everything you need to know about service dogs.* American Kennel Club. https://www.akc.org/expert-advice/training/service dog-training-101/#:~:text=A%20service%20dog%20is%20a

What is a wolf pack mentality? (2008, July 30). HowStuffWorks. https://animals.howstuffworks.com/mammals/wolf-pack-mentality.htm

Browse Free HD Images of Dapper Dog Gentleman With Bowtie On Black Background. (n.d.). In *Burst.*

https://burst.shopify.com/photos/dapper-dog-gentleman-with-bowtie-on-black-background?q=dog

Browse Free HD Images of The Face Of A Sled Dog Sprinkled With Snowflakes. (n.d.). In *Burst.* https://burst.shopify.com/photos/the-face-of-a-sled-dog-sprinkled-with-snowflakes?q=dog

Free Adorable Dog Desires Treat Photo — High Res Pictures. (n.d.). In *Burst.* https://burst.shopify.com/photos/adorable-dog-desires-treat?q=dog

Free Pug Dog & Pumpkin Photo — High Res Pictures. (n.d.). In *Burst.* https://burst.shopify.com/photos/pug-dog-pumpkin?q=dog

High Res Blanket Pug Looks To Future Picture — Free Images. (n.d.). In *Burst.* https://burst.shopify.com/photos/blanket-pug-looks-to-future?q=dog